The Footprints of Jesus' Twelve

American University Studies

Series VII
Theology and Religion

Vol. 7

PETER LANG
New York · Berne · Frankfurt am Main

Heinz O. Guenther

The Footprints of Jesus' Twelve in Early Christian Traditions

A Study in the Meaning of Religious Symbolism

PETER LANG
New York · Berne · Frankfurt am Main

Library of Congress Cataloging in Publication Data

Guenther, Heinz O., 1926–
   The Footprints of Jesus' Twelve in Early Christian
Traditions.

   (American University Studies.   Series VII, Theology
and Religion; vol. 7)
   Bibliography: p.
   Includes indexes.
   1. Apostles.   2. Bible. N.T. Luke – Criticism,
Interpretation, etc.   3. Bible. N.T. Acts – Criticism,
Interpretation, etc.   4. Apostolic Fathers.   5. Twelve
(The number)   I. Title.   II. Series: American University
Studies.   Series VII, Theology and Religion; v. 7.
BS2440.G84   1985   225.6'7   84-48032
ISBN 0-8204-0164-1
ISSN 0740-0446

CIP-Kurztitelaufnahme der Deutschen Bibliothek

Guenther, Heinz O.: The Footprints of Jesus' Twelve in Early
Christian Traditions: A Study in the Meaning
of Religious Symbolism / Heinz O. Guenther. –
New York; Berne; Frankfurt am Main: Lang,
1985.
   (American University Studies: Ser. 7, Theology
   and Religion; Vol. 7)
   ISBN 0-8204-0164-1

NE: American University Studies / 07

© Peter Lang Publishing, Inc., New York 1985

Printed by Lang Druck, Inc., Liebefeld/Berne (Switzerland)

PREFACE

The beginnings of this study on the origin and the
religious significance of the variegated Christian twelve
system date back to the time when I taught New Testament
studies at Kwansei Gakuin University in Nishinomiya, Japan.
The work was continued and finally completed in Toronto,
Canada. The material presented in this publication is the
summary version of two unpublished essays on the subject
matter initially designed as teaching material for students
enrolled in my graduate seminars. The first of these was
written in honour of the former Principal of Emmanuel College, William O. Fennell, as a token of gratitude for his
friendship and advice in my early years of teaching at Emmanuel College of Victoria University. The theological
dialogue with this scholar has always been a rich source of
encouragement for me. The second essay was an attempt to
put the conclusions of the first in perspective. The purpose of the revision of these two essays was not to be ex-
haustive of the literature on the Christian twelve. The
intention to demonstrate the complexity of the symbolic
power endemic to the Christian twelve concept has been the
determinative factor in my selection of the literature consulted here. The three twelve traditions examined in this
study have undoubtedly contributed to the symbolic significance the Christian twelve have come to exercise in the
later New Testament writings. Their symbolic power, however, is much greater than the sum total of these three
traditions might suggest. To secure a sufficient flow of
the argument, the discussion of several controversial details relevant to the study had to be relegated to the
footnotes.

Two sources of encouragement deserve special mention.
First, I benefitted greatly from the constant stimuli provided by colleagues and students participating in the

Advanced Degree Seminar of the Biblical Department within
the Toronto School of Theology. Second, the students who
took my courses on the apostolate in the early church have
been, in many ways, my challengers and teachers. They all
deserve my thanks.

I am pleased to express my appreciation to the Presi-
dent of Victoria University, Dr. Goldwin S. French, and to
the Principal of Emmanuel College, Dr. C. Douglas Jay, for
supporting the preparation of the manuscript with a contri-
bution from the Emmanuel College Research Fund. I am most
grateful to Dr. C. Douglas Jay for negotiating with the
United Church of Canada Book Publishing Fund, and to Rever-
end Randolph L. Naylor for the Fund's generous assistance in
covering the printing expenses of this publication.

My deepest gratitude is to my wife Anneliese for providing an 'island of peace' amidst the routines of an otherwise hectic life of teaching and study. Without her steady
support this study would never have been completed.

June 1984   Heinz O. Guenther

TABLE OF CONTENTS

PART ONE

THE PROBLEM

The puzzling fact that among all the New Testament writers
only Luke has advocated the apostolate of the twelve disciples of the earthly Jesus cannot be removed by arguments
from silence. To contend that those biblical writers who
did not speak about the institution of the twelve apostles
may have been fully aware nonetheless of their foundational
significance is to elevate guesswork to the rank of sources.
Any investigation of the available texts becomes superfluous
if suppositions are allowed to be the leading principle of
research. That the viewpoint of the researcher definitely
determines his understanding of the available sources is too
obvious to be seriously disputed. But still this does not
justify the attempt to let the researcher's viewpoint dictate the results of his investigation. The late appearance
of the apostolate of the twelve in Christian literature is
not adequately explained if the knowledge of the institution
is simply read into those writings which do not speak of them.
Whatever the dogmatic inclinations of the individual scholar,
the fact remains that the distinct group of only twelve apostles is first introduced into the written early Christian
tradition by the evangelist Luke. Even in the two Lukan
writings themselves the group seems to have grown in significance. While the final edition of the Lukan gospel,
perhaps completed in Asia Minor,[1] mentions the twelve apostles only 6 times,[2] the second century book of Acts[3] refers
to them 26 times.[4] Even if we should agree that Luke's shift
of interest from the earthly ministry of Jesus to the expansion of the church may have had some bearing on this numerical
distribution, the increase of their significance in the book
of Acts still remains rather conspicuous. The mention of the
twelve apostle college in the Lukan writings, along with the
appearance of 'the twelve' in other New Testament books, constitutes a series of very delicate problems of chronology and

tradition-historical interrelation. It would be rash to attempt to solve them all en bloc. In the first part of this
study we will deal with

    a.   the significance of the twelve apostles in Luke's
        theology;

    b.   their appearance in the writings of the apostolic
        fathers;

    c.   the synoptic (and pre-synoptic) view of the twelve;
        and

    d.   the twelve in the Q Source.

An examination of the generally shared assumption that Jesus
had summoned a group of twelve disciples during his earthly
ministry will conclude the discussion of the first part. An
attempt will be made in the second part to interpret the earlier findings in terms of the underlying religious symbolism.

CHAPTER I
THE TENSION BETWEEN LUKE AND THE APOSTOLIC FATHERS

The twelve apostolic office-holders do not only make their
first appearance in the Lukan writings. They also constitute one of the theological themes running through the two
compositions of the evangelist. In almost programmatic
fashion, and for the first time in early church history,
Luke sets down in Acts the criteria for what he considers
the qualifications of legitimate Christian apostleship.
Only those qualify for this highest office in the church
who had accompanied Jesus "during all the time that the
Lord Jesus went in and out among [his disciples], beginning from the baptism of John, until the day when he was
taken up . . . ."[5] Not the privilege of a heavenly post-
Easter revelation but their call by the earthly Jesus, and
their full participation in the earthly history of Jesus
alone distinguishes, in Luke's view, an apostle from a
follower of Jesus. For Luke, the twelve apostles out-
shine all other earthly eyewitnesses because they not only
came up with Jesus "from Galilee to Jerusalem"[6] but also
ate and drank with the Lord after he rose from the dead."[7]
In view of the rigidity of these qualifications for apostleship, it comes as no surprise that only two candidates
were available for the apostolic position vacated by Judas,
the "guide to those who had arrested Jesus."[8] After all,
who among the early disciples of Jesus could possibly be
said to have been with the Lord during "all" the time (ἐν
παντὶ χρόνῳ) from his baptism to his ascension?

The informed reader of Acts cannot fail to note that
Luke's precisely defined requirements for apostleship speak,
by implication, against the apostleship of the man to whom
the evangelist devoted more than half of his second composition. Paul neither accompanied the earthly Jesus nor ever
ate and drank with him after his resurrection. Not once
therefore is Paul called in Acts an equal of the twelve

apostles. Whenever Luke attributes the title 'apostle' to him (14:4.14), he makes it very clear that he means 'messengership' and not genuine apostleship. In these two references, Paul appears side by side with Barnabas, another non-apostolic subordinate of the great Jerusalem twelve. H. Conzelmann has elaborated upon the positive side of the Lukan image of the non-apostolic Paul. The evangelist, he says, did not intend to slight the great missionary of the early church. Rather, his own interest in Paul as a link between the church's ideal Jerusalem time and the present accounts for the latter's place "outside the apostolic circle."[9] All this shows that the book of Acts is indeed a "combination of ideas and theories," as K. Lake put it,[10] and Luke's tendentious portrayal of Paul is in itself sufficient evidence that these 'theories' were not prompted by the evangelist's concern for historical accuracy but rather by his theological premises.[11]

As said before, in Luke's Acts the apostolate of the twelve is rooted in Jesus' earthly history. Chosen by the earthly Jesus from among his many followers (Lk. 6:13), they are part of Jesus' earthly ministry. Without the twelve apostles the church could, in Luke's judgment, not set out on its great evangelistic journey into the world. Even the miraculous outpouring of the Holy Spirit had to wait until the impaired number of the twelve had been fully restored by the election of the obscure figure of Matthias. As the "only normative bearers" of the apostolic tradition[12] and the "guarantors of the Church's teaching,"[13] the twelve apostles are, according to Acts, commissioned to govern and to administer the church in the capacity of authoritative leaders, teachers, missionaries and miracle-workers. It must be noted, however, that Luke, the first early Christian spokesman advocating the importance of an indispensable apostolic tradition in the church, was not the initiator of the later ecclesiastical theory of the apostolic succession. Luke was much more concerned with

the continuity of the tradition than the continuity of office.
'Succession of tradition', not 'apostolic succession' was on
Luke's mind when he wrote the book of Acts.[14] The tradition
of apostolic succession was most probably fashioned, in the
later parts of the second century or early third century, to
parallel "the Jewish lists of High Priests,"[15] as A. Ehrhardt
has shown persuasively.

It is beyond any shadow of doubt that the book of Acts
is the only New Testament document which elevated the twelve
to the position of unequalled apostolic leaders within the
church. Does this make Luke the founder of the so-called
twelve-apostle tradition[16] or was he only the chief interpreter of an already existing tradition?[17] Do we have evidence that Luke was the collector of reliable information on
the twelve preserved by the church for historical (or theological) reasons?[18] These are the issues to which we will
now turn our attention in the examination of the available
source materials. Luke's attempt to remove Paul from among
the church's genuine apostles by setting down qualifications
for this high office which only the disciples of the earthly
Jesus could fulfil is without parallels in early Christian
literature. Significantly, the apostolic fathers do not show
any acquaintance with Luke's all-out transformation of the
apostle Paul into a loyal subordinate of first the Jerusalem
twelve and later the Jerusalem elders.[19] It is not even
certain why they are so secretive about the institution of
the twelve apostles. Did the fierce struggle of the second
century churches with gnosticism divert their attention from
Luke's twelve or does their nonchalance with regard to this
matter imply that in their day the book of Acts had not been
in circulation yet?[20]

Occupied with the refutation of what he calls heretic
"evil doctrines,"[21] Ignatius of Antioch, for instance, never
tired of highlighting the prominence of the episcopacy for
the life of his church. The current bishop is for him "as
the Lord himself"[22] and only those who live "in subjection

to him"[23] live a truly good life. Absolute obedience to the
bishop was for Ignatius the only viable weapon to protect the
Christian identity against any pollution by the "evil odour
of the doctrine of the Prince of this world."[24] It is not
surprising that Ignatius' high view of the bishop even affected his references to 'the apostles'. It was the believer's
attitude to the bishop which determined for Ignatius the believer's stance to the apostles. Those obedient to the epis-
copus are, by implication, declared to be "of one mind with
the apostles in the power of Jesus Christ."[25] By virtue of
their own obedience to Jesus, who is the bishop of all,"[26]
the apostles are, in Ignatius' judgment, archetypes of exemplary Christian loyalty. The essential thing here is that
Ignatius made the apostles inaccessible to the Christian
church. The local bishop is for him the only gate through
which to approach these ancient figures of Christian piety.
No direct appeal can be made to them. In giving heed to the
bishop, the believers are assured of both their participation
in the apostolic church and their spiritual relationship with
these most venerable figures of old.[27]

Whom had Ignatius in mind when he referred so generally
to 'the apostles'? The student of Acts is struck by Ignatius'
complete silence about the exclusive group of the 'twelve
apostles'. W. Schmithals' conclusion that Ignatius may have
had in mind contemporary Christian (gnostic) missionaries
wandering about in Syria or Egypt[28] is ingenious but without
any real support in the writings themselves. The contemporary
missionaries are called God's 'foot soldiers', a technical
term (πέζοι)[29] borrowed from Roman military language, or God's
couriers (θεοδρόμοι).[30] These terms have no gnostic under-
tones. What is important here is that apostleship is not
accorded to these missionaries. Ignatius' distance from
Luke's apostle concept is nonetheless manifest in his reference to the apostles Peter and Paul. "I do not order you
as did Peter and Paul; they were apostles. . . ."[31] Luke's
undisguised exclusion of Paul from apostleship eliminates the

book of Acts as the source for a statement which takes Paul's
apostleship for granted. To read Ignatius' espousal of Peter's
and Paul's apostleship as a suppressed criticism of Luke's low-
keyed portrayal of Paul is not convincing either. Criticism of
a composition otherwise not mentioned at all is certainly not
an effective form of criticism. Unacquainted with any claim
that the twelve are the only legitimate apostles in the church,
Ignatius presents a view of apostleship which Luke tried very
hard to dispute.

Similarly to Ignatius, Clemens Romanus too speaks of
"apostles" who "received the gospel for our sakes from the
Lord" and who went out to preach the kingdom "filled with
confidence by the resurrection of our Lord Jesus Christ, and
confirmed in faith by the word of God."[32] However, his unspecified references to 'the good apostles Peter and Paul'[33]
demonstrate his ignorance of the Lukan portrait of Paul. Is
it really possible to say that Clemens was fully cognizant of
Luke's institution of the twelve apostles but still generous
enough to include Paul among them?

Polycarp's preoccupation with the spiritual significance
of the Pauline letters as well as the work of "the blessed and
glorious Paul"[34] prevented him from dealing with any of the
other early Christian writings known in his day. Only in
passing did he refer to "the apostles who brought us the gospel,"[35] calling upon the Christian community always to keep
in mind the endurance manifest "in Paul . . . and in the other
apostles."[36] No mention of 'the twelve apostles' is made in
the writings of the bishop of Smyrna. The possibility cannot
be excluded that Polycarp was not at all thinking of the twelve
but only of 'the apostles before Paul' (Gal. 1:17; Rm. 16:7) or
perhaps even of contemporary missionary preachers. For the
latter use of the term the Didache is a good illustration.

Speaking of "apostles and prophets,"[37] the Didache calls
upon the Christian communities to receive every visiting apostle "as the Lord"[38] and to "let him stay" one or two days.[39]
The duration of such a visit is even the yardstick by which to

distinguish between true and false contemporary apostles. The community is asked to look after them for only two days. "But if he should stay three days" or even "ask for money, he is a false prophet."[40] The fact that in the judgment of the Didache 'apostles and prophets' may be capable of bad conduct determines the meaning of these references. As K. Lake aptly put it, the apostle is for Didache merely "a Christian missionary and nothing more."[41] It is worth remembering that wandering apostles are also familiar to the writer of the Book of Revelation (Rev. 2:2). One must certainly not read the Didache's view of apostleship into Polycarp's letter. In fact, much can be said for the view that Polycarp did not know anything at all about contemporary apostles. Nonetheless, it is quite clear that neither Polycarp nor the Didache was familiar with Luke's tightly knit twelve apostle concept, let alone with his exclusion of Paul from their ranks. The same holds true of the Book of Revelation (Rev. 18:20; 21:14) a writing which offers a rather spiritualized view of 'the twelve apostles'. The idea of the celestial twelve whose names are engraved forever upon the walls of the Jerusalem above may indeed have been fashioned on a pesher on Isaiah 54:11-12, as D. Flusser has suggested.[42] However, in terms of content, no affinity exists between the Book of Revelation and the Book of Acts.

By contrast, Barnabas had the twelve apostles in mind when he spoke of the "twelve" preaching the gospel to the "twelve tribes of Israel."[43] However, the absence of any mention of Paul in Barnabas' letter does not suggest that he derived his knowledge of the twelve from the Lukan writings. It cannot go unnoticed furthermore that in contrast to Luke, Barnabas did not refer to the office or institution of the twelve apostles. He speaks rather casually of them, referring to "the apostles" in chapter five, while mentioning "the twelve" in chapter eight. These references are reminiscent of Mark's gospel but certainly not of Acts.

A strong case can definitely not be made for the affinity between Luke's highly sophisticated twelve apostle concept and

the casual references of the apostolic fathers to apostles.
To say the least, no intimate relationship exists between
Luke's enumeration of only twelve indispensable and irreplaceable office-bearers exercising a foundational role in
the growing church universal[44] and the fathers' vague and
unprecise comments on the exemplary significance of an unspecified group of so-called 'apostles'. Had the fathers
known Luke's Acts they would hardly have been able to speak
so unreflectively of past and/or current apostles.[45] Neither
could they have mentioned 'the twelve' without acknowledging
the work of Paul.[46] The distinctness of Luke's apostle concept is thus unparalleled in early Christian literature
between 100 - 150 C.E. Whether Luke should be called the
founder of the twelve apostle tradition (G. Klein) or whether
he only made use of a "scantily attested but . . . already
existent" tradition by further elevating the designation
'apostle' "to the level of a legal terminus technicus"
(W. Schmithals),[47] can here be left in abeyance. As we have
seen before, the scarcity of the references to 'the twelve
apostles' in the apostolic fathers indicates Luke's highly
creative role in the shaping of this tradition. The evidence for the existence of a twelve apostle tradition in
either Luke's vicinity or in the pre-Lukan church is very
thin. Is it surprising that scholars trying to conclude
that Luke must nonetheless have derived his twelve concept
from the existing church tradition had to take recourse to
a good many arguments from silence? Not every researcher
is able to base his investigation on so weak a foundation.

Luke's creation of a numerically closed group of twelve un-
matchable apostolic office-holders was not a creation ex nihilo.
The elusiveness of the boundaries between Jesus' pre-Easter and
post-Easter 'apostles' in the writings of the apostolic fathers
indeed suggests that Luke played a leading role in establishing
the twelve as the only apostolic eyewitnesses to and guarantors
of the Jesus tradition.[48] The emphasis of Acts on the foundational significance of the numerically limited body of the
earthly Jesus' twelve disciples for the church universal undoubtedly highlights Luke's own theological response to both
the delay of the parousia and the growth of the church in Asia
Minor and Greece. However, Luke still did not start from
nothing when he shaped his unique version of the twelve apostolic office-holders in relation to whom all others, including
Paul, are of secondary rank.

The composition of the book of Acts was prompted by Luke's
intention to create a chronologically correlated story fit to
fulfil two basic functions in the life of the church. The
story was firstly to account for the church's unprecedented
expansion into the Hellenistic world, and secondly to support
the growing church in its attempt to refute what Luke thought
to be innovative yet highly disintegrating 'Christian' teachings.[49] In his endeavour to introduce some measure of doc-
trinal stability into his precarious church situation, Luke
could fall back on a list of twelve names (Mk. 3:16-19) which
he had found in the Markan gospel. The list itself was not a
Markan creation either but was part of Mark's own source materials. Mark had incorporated these twelve into his gospel
without attributing to them any special status. In contra-
distinction to Luke's description of the twelve apostles, the
Markan twelve are not office-holders at all. As E. Best put
it, "we cannot . . . say that Mark stresses the position of
the Twelve as apostles. . . . In Mark's eyes the Twelve are

typical believers rather than officials of the Church."[50]
Neither does Mark regard them as founders of the church.[51]
Mark conceived of his present as the time of mourning over
the absence of Jesus, the bridegroom (Mk. 2:19). Positively
put, as a relatively short interval (Mk. 13:7) between Jesus'
resurrection and his reappearance in glory (Mk. 9:1; 13:30)
the present provides the twelve in the second gospel with un-
foreseen opportunities for mission (Mk. 13:10). The interchangeability in Mark's gospel of the designation 'disciples'
(οἱ μαθηταί) with that of the twelve (οἱ δώδεκα),[52] along with
the emphasis on their generally defined commission 'to preach
and to cast out demons',[53] further affirms what we have said
before. For Mark the twelve are nothing other than fully-
fledged disciple-missionaries. E. Best again put it succinctly when he says that the task of the Markan twelve is
"in fact laid on the whole Church."[54] Nothing is said in
Mk. 3:13-19 about the role of the twelve as leaders "governing
a community," as G. Theissen has claimed in his interpretation of
the passage.[55] Nonetheless, the introduction of a pre-Markan
name list (Mk. 3:16-19)[56] into his portrayal of Jesus' Galilean ministry now forced the second evangelist to accommodate
the twelve to all those strands of his source material which
originally did not exhibit any familiarity with them. The so-
called δώδεκα passages[57] are therefore all "the secondary editorial work of Mark."[58] They represent Mark's attempt to give
the twelve a place within the whole body of traditions which
originally had nothing to do with them, and which still resist
their presence most tangibly.[59] In a recent study, E. Best
advocated the partisan view that 'the twelve' had already occupied a firm place in the pre-Markan tradition.[60] It is
interesting to note, however, that in doing so he nonetheless
underlines Mark's theological disinterest in them. Best concludes his study by affirming that Mark was "not basically
interested in the twelve."[61] He observes that in the second
gospel the twelve were "not . . . the link between Jesus and
the post-resurrection church in the transmission of his

teaching."[62] Neither were they for Mark "an inner circle" in contrast to the "outer circle of the disciples."[63] The men whom E. Best tried to find rooted in the pre-Markan tradition merely are, he states, "full-time missionaries."[64] Did E. Best succeed in his attempt to prove that these twelve 'missionaries' had been an integral part of Mark's traditional material? Almost against his own will, his study illustrates how difficult, if not impossible, it is to anchor them in the pre-Markan tradition. All E. Best's exegetical analysis establishes is that the existence of explicit references to the twelve in the pre-Markan material should not be ruled out on principle.[65] It is easier to assume, says Best, that the δώδεκα-references, most admittedly in largely redactional context,[66] had a place in the pre-Markan materials.[67] But is it convincing to argue that while the context of the δώδεκα-passages is largely redactional, the δώδεκα-designation itself should be regarded as traditional? And what should one say of Best's observation that although Mark's use of δώδεκα in Mk. 14:17, for instance, may be redactional,[68] the reference to the twelve itself was probably forced on Mark by the tradition . . ."?[69] A very remote possibility does not yet make a good and plausible probability!

It can be assumed that the Markan references to the twelve provided Luke with the raw material by means of which he was able to hammer out his own apostle concept. This is of course not to say that the Markan material itself prompted the creation of Luke's twelve apostles. In his struggle with Christian splinter groups,[70] Luke would have given much if he had found, as J. Knox aptly put it, "some document worthily representing the authority of all the Twelve."[71] All he found in Mark were a few casual remarks about a group of twelve disciple-missionaries with no theological significance attributed to them. E. Best again put it well when he states that the second evangelist did not make "anything of the number twelve in relation to the twelve; he did not connect the number twelve to any of the Old Testament 'twelve' concepts."[72] K. Lake's suggestion

that for Mark the twelve were "not an official class in a new
society,"[73] is not only to the point but also indirectly affirmed by Matthew's gospel. The first evangelist, who had
access to the same source materials available also to Luke,
did not discern any specific theological interest in the twelve
on the part of Mark. The δώδεκα are for Matthew merely archetypal figures of discipleship.[74] Throughout Matthew's gospel
these twelve disciples are prepared to pledge what G. Bornkamm
called unconditional "allegiance to Jesus and his teaching,"
and to learn constantly from him.[75] Should Mk. 6:30 be the
source of Mt. 14:12b, which is possible, then Matthew would
even have highlighted his total disinterest in 'the apostles'
by eliminating the only truly Markan reference to them.[76]
Matthew's single reference to the 'twelve apostles' (Mt. 10:2)
is too precarious to be counted as proof-text for the existence
of a twelve-apostle institution in Matthew's day. Matthew's
reference to "the names of the twelve apostles" (Mt. 10:2) is
so general that the text of his copy of the Markan gospel cannot be reconstructed from it. Whether or not the controversial
and most likely Lukan-inspired 'whom also he named apostles'
was in Matthew's copy of Mark cannot be inferred from Mt. 10:2.[77]

Given the textual weakness of the Sinai-Syriac side-
reading which mentions 'twelve disciples',[78] Matthew's failure
to attribute any specific authority to his 'twelve apostles'
indicates sufficiently that they were for him without any theological import (cf. Mt. 26:20). They merely represented, as
G.D. Kilpatrick affirms, "figures of the past."[79] Matthew's
gospel thus is strong evidence for the fact that Mark cannot
be regarded as the stimulus behind Luke's theological twelve-
apostle tradition.

The Markan gospel was not the only source available to
the third evangelist. If Luke's twelve apostolic office-
holders are theologically speaking poles apart from Mark's
rank and file missionary twelve, can the Document Q be claimed
as the source of information for Luke's twelve apostles? In
his detailed study of the Q texts, S. Schulz pointed out the

intimate relationship between the apocalyptic consciousness
of the Q circles and the equally strong apocalyptic orientation
of the Hellenistic Jewish-Christian apostolate.[80] Did the emphasis of several Q texts on the community's sense of mission
suggest to Luke the creation of a twelve-apostle tradition?

Given the complexity of the Q Source, which cannot be
reviewed here,[81] the strong missionary concern imprinted on
quite a number of Q texts cannot fail to strike the eye of
the reader. The Q version of the Great Commission, for instance,[82] encourages the Q group to pray that 'hired free
harvesters'[83] be continually 'sent' into the fields ripe for
the last great harvest of God (Lk. 10:2/Mt. 9:38). It is
significant that not only this Q text, but all the other relevant Q passages too, use the LXX terminus technicus ἀποστέλλειν (and not the general term πέμπειν) when speaking of
the Q mission. This has definitely some weight, even though
the distinction between the two terms should not lead to the
kind of separation in meaning which K. Rengstorf seems to
advocate.[84] Similarly to John the Baptist (Lk. 7:27/Mt. 11:10),
the Jewish Christian harvesters are sent unprotected into a
hostile Jewish environment (Lk. 10:3/Mt. 10:16), proclaiming
the imminence of God's kingdom (Lk. 10:9/Mt. 10:7) and sharing
in the divine mission of Jesus (Lk. 10:16/Mt. 10:40). The Q
missionaries are not appointed to administer the church under
the guidance of the Holy Spirit. They are sent (ἀποστέλλεσθαι)
to invite the unrepenting Jewish Torah community (Lk. 14:17/
Mt. 22:3) which, in the judgment of the Q theologians, has
already irredeemably lost the privilege of being called to the
great banquet of God (Lk. 13:34/Mt. 23:37). Are these five Q
texts with their admittedly very strong emphasis on 'sentness'[85] the missing link between Luke and a seminal pre-Lukan
apostle concept?

The conceptual difference between the missionary consciousness of Q, on the one hand, and that of the synoptic
twelve, on the other hand, is still so great that any attempt
to link the Q community harvesters to the twelve apostles

cannot but fail to convince. To begin with, granted the common element of sentness in both Q and Mark, Mark's ever-wavering and imperceptive twelve preacher-exorcists cannot be compared with the Q community disciples who, as Theodore J. Weeden accurately put it, do not "lack anything in visual and conceptual perception."[86] Needless to say, we compare here only the concepts, without suggesting Mark's knowledge of the Q Source.[87] The Q missionaries and Luke's twelve apostles have nothing in common either. While Luke's twelve continue to carry out their leadership tasks in Jerusalem even in the times of persecution (Acts 8:1), the Jewish Christian Q disciples are sent 'as lambs in the midst of [equally Jewish] wolves' (Lk. 10:3/Mt. 10:16).[88] The 'sentness'-concept of Q thus does not connect well with Luke's idea of twelve apostolic office-holders.

In addition, in terms of terminology, Luke's favourite apostolos-designation cannot readily be derived from Q. The only reference to 'apostle' within a Q context (Lk. 11:49/ Mt. 23:34) is most likely of Lukan origin. Significantly, scholars who claim the reference to 'apostles' for Q,[89] still had to admit that this wisdom saying, presumably of non-Christian origin, did not at all speak of Christian 'apostles' but rather, in analogy with the 'prophets' of Lk. 11:49, of unspecified Old Testament messengers.[90] Such conclusion does not yield much for our inquiry, for the conceptual gap between Luke and Q has now only been shifted from the New to the Old Testament. The so-called Old Testament apostle-messengers allegedly mentioned in Q (Lk. 11:49 par.) are even farther away from Luke's office-holders than is Q's own ἀποστέλλειν-concept. Aside from this, is it really convincing to argue that Matthew would have replaced an original Q reference to 'apostles' with the rather elusive designation of 'wise men' (σοφοί) (Mt. 23:34), an appellation which otherwise does not appear at all in Matthean redactional contexts but is attested only in Q passages (Lk. 10:21/Mt. 11:25)?

In sum, the strong apocalyptic missionary consciousness
of Q, along with the emphasis of the Source on the community's
sense of being sent into the hostile surrounding culture, does
not bridge the gap between the Q messenger-harvesters and
Luke's Christian supervisory and leadership exercising apostles. The Q concept of 'sentness', not unlike the Markan
references to the twelve, was thus at best only the rude clay
by which Luke, confronted with an unstable church situation,
fashioned his twelve apostle tradition. There is no indica-
tion that in shaping this tradition he was guided by the immediate concerns of the Q mission. It cannot be overlooked,
however, that Q had an interesting 'twelve concept' of its
own, a concept unrelated to Luke's twelve apostles yet still
historically more persuasive than that found in either Mark
or Paul.

CHAPTER III
THE TRACES OF THE TWELVE IN THE PRE-SYNOPTIC
AND OTHER INDEPENDENT TRADITIONS

Luke's share in the transformation of the twelve Markan disciples into twelve uniquely appointed apostolic office-holders
has been under scrutiny in the preceding sections of this
study. What has not been discussed yet is why long before
Luke, and indeed even before Mark, differing 'twelve' concepts
had emerged in various strands of the Christian tradition.
A brief investigation into these concepts will make us aware
of the theological concerns behind the Christian twelve tradition.

i. The irreconcilable differences[91] in the four synoptic disciple lists[92] may indeed be due to the novelistic idiosyncra-
sies of either the synoptic writers themselves or their pre-
synoptic counterparts.[93] Nonetheless, the fact remains that
these lists contain twelve names, Judas always being directly
or indirectly included. What inspired the pre-Markan church
to put down twelve names? Why 'twelve'? In Mark's gospel, the
twelve are missionaries accompanying the earthly Jesus during
his Galilean and Jerusalem ministry. Were the twelve of the
pre-Markan lists missionaries too? The point here is that a
redactionally reframed and interpretively revised early twelve
concept left its marks on the Markan tradition.

ii. Quite another twelve concept is found in the pre-Pauline
strands of the Christian tradition. It is possible that early
church political interests may originally have prompted the
listing of the Lord's visitation to (mutually competing?) individual leaders or leadership groups within the early post-
Easter communities.[94] In this event Paul would only have welded
together various circulating pre-Pauline traditions.[95] Whatever the relationship between 'the twelve' (1 Cor. 15:5) and
'all the apostles' (1 Cor. 15:7) may have been, an appearance

of the Lord is accorded here to a group of twelve specifically mentioned post-Easter members of the early Christian
community. Since Paul nowhere intimates any acquaintance
with these twelve,[96] they cannot readily be identified with
'the apostles before Paul' (Gal. 1:17), some of whom he still
knew personally (Rm. 16:7).[97] The inclusion of Judas in the
synoptic twelve lists suggests the independence of the pre-
Markan concept from that of the pre-Pauline formula. A post-
Easter visitation of the Lord to his pre-Easter twelve is in-
conceivable because it would make Judas a part of the post-
Easter group. The Lukan Matthias story furthermore is so
late that it cannot be made to bridge the gap between the
two traditions. It is interesting to note that scholars trying to reconcile the two twelve concepts with one another had
to pile up one hypothesis upon another in order to explain
away Judas' disturbing presence from among the group mentioned
in 1 Cor. 15:5. The hypothesis that the post-Easter twelve of
1 Cor. 15:5 had been an institution frequently inconvenienced
by vacancies[98] had here to support the first hypothesis claiming the identity of the pre-Markan twelve with the corporate
body of the pre-Pauline twelve. Can it go unnoticed that already the copyists saw the futility of any such attempt at
reconciliation? Presupposing the identity of both groups, the
copyists of several manuscripts did not hesitate to reduce the
pre-Pauline twelve to a body of only eleven members.[99] But
this attempt at harmonization seriously violates the integrity
of the otherwise undamaged text. Why should one try to identify the two traditions when the identification raises problems which can only be solved by a serious interference with
the text? Both the pre-Markan and the pre-Pauline account
indeed speak of 'the twelve'. But the mention of the same
number does still not justify the identification of the two
groups. The reference to 'the twelve' in these two traditions
does in itself not imply that the relationship between the two
was an unbroken one, historically or theologically.

iii. The significance of the number 'twelve' within the Q community is highlighted by a third early Christian twelve concept. Lk. 22:28-30/Mt. 19:28 is a prophetic saying[100] which assures the Q group of its fullest participation in the courtrooms of the future Son of Man. As rightly appointed eschatological judge-figures the twelve (whoever they may have been) are promised to sit on (twelve)[101] judgment thrones assisting the Son of Man in the concluding acts of a cataclysmic apocalyptic drama. The two versions of the Q saying, both inserted into different Markan contexts,[102] have ten basic words in common.[103] Two further striking conceptual similarities[104] support the generally shared assumption that the saying was part of the Q tradition.[105] The 'eschatological promise' (H.C. Kee) reflects the strained relationship which by the middle of the first century must have obtained between the Jewish Christian Q community on the one hand, and the equally Jewish (Torah) communities on the other. The rejection of the Christian message by the Jewish majority most probably gave birth to this assuring prophetic saying which ascribes an important eschatological role in God's Last Judgment to the Jewish Christian Q minority. The inner-Jewish character of the controversy does not allow us to characterize the saying as 'anti-Jewish', any more than the appointment of ten Qumran judges by the Damascus group was anti-Jewish.[106]

The promised judgmental role of the Q twelve separates them sharply from both their synoptic and pre-Pauline counterparts. Luke's twelve are ecclesiastical authority figures exercising an administrative as well as a spiritual function within the contemporary church. Mark's twelve are sent out to preach (and to cast out demons) during Jesus' earthly ministry. Paul's twelve are witnesses of the Lord's post-Easter appearance. The gap between these groups of twelve and that of Q is so deep that even the clarification of the controversial question as to whether the original Q saying was addressed

to twelve individual community leaders[107] or to the community
as a whole[108] would not bring these groups any closer together.
Even if the 'ὑμεῖς' (you who have followed me) of the original
Q saying should signify the same group of persons envisaged by
1 Cor. 15:5, their function still separates them most deci-
sively from one another. The Q twelve fulfil neither a supervisory ecclesiastical nor a missionary function. As the ter-
minological affinity of the Q saying with the intertestamental
writings shows,[109] the function of the Q twelve is apocalyptic-
eschatological.

Of further importance here is that the Q twelve, who are
much more positively portrayed than the Markan twelve,[110] are
not envisioned to function in the present. The fulfillment of
the promise lies so much in the future that they could not
even prepare themselves in any tangible fashion for their future task. Luke's twelve have a good measure of real authority in the contemporary church (Acts 6:6; 11:1f; 15:6). As
his earthly companions, Mark's twelve are always with Jesus,
receiving full instruction in the secrets of the kingdom which
they never really grasp (Mk. 3:14; 4:10.34 et al.). A vision
of the Lord is attributed to the post-Easter twelve of pre-
Pauline provenance (1 Cor. 15:5). By contrast, the Q twelve
can only spend their day waiting for the temporal end of history. No visionary or missionary action on their part can
usher in the Last Judgment. The twelve concept of Q thus represents a claim rather than a function. Conscious of being
the true remnant of Israel,[111] the Q twelve looked forward to
the time when God would make them sit next to him in the Son
of Man's Great Hall. Since their task, void of any real significance in the present, consisted only of 'waiting', they
could not survive the continual delay of the Lord's coming.
No one can wait forever.

Whether twelve individual community leaders or the corporate representation of the community's consciousness, the Q
twelve did not play a significant role within the Q circles.
Only one out of the more than sixty Q texts listed by Siegfried

Schulz refers to them. However, what is important to note in our context is that 'the twelve' have indeed left their stamp on three different early Christian traditions: the pre-Markan, the pre-Pauline and the Q tradition. In these three post-Easter traditions, which emerged independently of each other, the key focus of attention is not at all on their roles as individuals. Admittedly, the pre-Markan tradition lists the names of twelve individuals. But the Markan gospel makes it plain that not one detail of their individual missionary activity was remembered by the later church. Throughout the whole gospel, 'the twelve' (sometimes 'the three') act together as a group. The appearance experience of the pre-Pauline twelve is also a group experience. The anonymous members of a group of twelve see the Lord. And finally, the Q twelve are also a body of judges who are promised to function in a most outstanding fashion in the Last Judgment. In view of this, is it likely that Jesus himself appointed these twelve who fulfil different functions in the tradition, without any detail about their individual activity being remembered by the early communities involved? To this question we now turn in conclusion of the first part of this study.

CONCLUSION

No a priori reason exists either for claiming or for disclaim-
ing the appointment of the twelve by Jesus himself. The absence of any supportive historical evidence theoretically
allows for both positions. Research into grey areas of this
type must begin by examining both the manner in which claims
have been made in the past and the motifs which may lie behind
them. Since the majority even of critical 20th century scholars have claimed that Jesus had already summoned a group of
'the twelve' during his earthly activity,[112] it will suffice
in this part of our investigation to deal only with the ways
in which distinguished researchers in this field have substan-
tiated their affirmations.

K. Lake, for instance, has argued that twelve carefully
chosen pre-Easter missionary companions of Jesus must be assumed to stand behind Mark's highly imaginary post-Easter
"special lieutenants" of the Lord,[113] a view reminiscent of
K. Holl's earlier assertion that "the twelve who were gathering together after the resurrection were those who had accompanied Jesus during his lifetime, belonging to the inner circle
of his followers."[114] But how does K. Lake substantiate these
far-reaching claims? Had the appointment of the twelve missionary disciples been altogether Mark's own theological creation, he says, then "it would surely be possible to see the
reasons for which [their appointment] was put [into the gos-
pel]."[115] Is this a cogent reason for suggesting their appointment by the earthly Jesus? Should it be impossible to
identify the theological reasons behind Mark's portrayal of the
twelve as missionaries?

The delay of the parousia prompted the church to provide
its missionaries with preaching material in the ever-extending
interim period between the resurrection and the expected end of
temporal history (Mk. 13:10). In the redactionally framed passage of Mk. 3:13-19, the pre-Markan twelve-disciple list therefore appears in the context of mission and preaching. Mark's

purpose to write his gospel for the <u>preaching</u> church prompted
him to present the twelve pre-Markan names redactionally as
the names of twelve archetypal missionary <u>preachers</u>. Had he
intended to write a story about the Last Judgment, he could as
readily have identified these twelve names with the twelve future judges mentioned, for instance, in the Q text of Mt. 19:28
par. It was not particularly difficult, furthermore, even to
transform them into twelve hallowed celestial yet exceedingly
passive figures whose glorious names John saw, in his vision,
carved on the permanence of the walls of the heavenly Jerusalem
(Rev. 21:14). The overall purpose of Mark's composition makes
it crystal-clear why the evangelist preferred to portray them
as missionaries, and not, as K. Lake himself rightly observed,
as "the foundation of a new church organization."[116] The missionary function of the twelve in Mark's gospel is so inti-
mately related to Mark's theology that an appointment by the
earthly Jesus himself can only be assumed if one is willing to
take theology for history.[117]

Not unlike K. Lake, J. Munck postulates that Luke's creation of the twelve-apostle institution[118] can safely be traced
back to the appointment of the twelve by the earthly Jesus.[119]
How did J. Munck arrive at this assuring conclusion? He assumes that in addition to the Markan source material, Luke must
have had access to a certain body of historical "information"[120] about the earthly role of the twelve. The information, Munck suggests, was not available to anyone except Luke.
This alleged body of (oral?) information, Munck assumes, may
be conjectured to lie behind Luke's theological construction
of the so-called Jerusalem "college" of apostles.[121]

Is the hypothesis of Luke's access to a body of otherwise unavailable information more tenable than K. Lake's assumption of a historical core in the Markan appointment story?
M. Dibelius,[122] H. Conzelmann,[123] E. Haenchen,[124]
Ch. H. Talbert,[125] and others have convincingly demonstrated
that Luke's whole Acts account (from Pentecost, Luke's image
of the Jerusalem church, the witness motif, Peter's leading

role in Gentile mission to the portrait of Paul etc.) is a
kerygmatic construct of its own. In view of this, is it
plausible to claim some historically valid information for
the legend of Judas' replacement by the otherwise entirely
unknown Matthias? We have already pointed out that neither
the biblical writers nor the apostolic fathers knew anything
of him. Can alleged 'evidence' which was neither available nor accessible to any other contemporary writer be
counted as historical evidence? It is generally agreed that
in all other areas of his work Luke was well able to produce
new Christian 'facts' on the basis of his own faith concerns.[126] Would those who allegedly informed him of the
function played by the twelve apostles not also have given
him some clues about the individual work of Matthias or the
earthly activity of the other 'apostles'? In Acts, Matthias'
sole function is to replace Judas. After the fulfillment of
this role he falls into oblivion. Is this an authentic role?
To say the least, the hypothesis regarding Luke's access to
certain otherwise unaccountable 'information' is, in the
light of Luke's whole Acts composition, not very persuasive.[127]
How strangely scholarly premises can dictate conclusions is
manifest in A. Polag's treatment of the Matthias story. On
the one hand, he acknowledges the redactional character of
the Lukan story about the appointment of the seven deacons
(Acts 6:1-6), while claiming, on the other hand, historical
authenticity for Matthias' promotion to the ranks of the
Jerusalem apostles.[128] Can one claim the one and reasonably
deny the other?

Moreover, it is interesting to note that scholars claiming the appointment of the twelve by the earthly Jesus have
always been troubled by the fact that none of the earliest
Christian writers seem to have known any of them personally.
J. Munck epitomizes the general dilemma well when he says that
the twelve must have disappeared even before the earliest
Christian mission ever really got under way.[129] No personal
knowledge of the twelve on the part of Paul, for instance, is

discernable in the letters.[130] The pre-Markan materials mention twelve individual names, but concrete details about their
activity apparently were no longer available to Mark. The
pre-Markan tradition remembered the person of Simon (the post-
Easter Peter), but biographical knowledge of any of the other
eleven disciples was not at the disposal of this tradition
either. This explains why Mark merely designated them as
'the twelve', a collective term more indicative of his lack
of information than of his admiration of their historical
roles and performance. Even if the Q saying of Mt. 19:28 par.
should have envisioned twelve individuals, the fact still remains that neither their individual names nor a report on their
activity appear in this early source. Would the church's mem-
ory of these men have faded away so completely if Jesus himself
had commissioned them to preach and cast out demons? Can
uniquely appointed individuals really disappear from the pages
of history without leaving the least trace of their work behind them?

The delicate question of the historicity of their appointment by the earthly Jesus is further highlighted by the
almost confusing diversity of their function in the earliest
source materials. The pre-Markan tradition represents them
as twelve names. Mark attributes these names in secondary
fashion to twelve missionaries. In Paul's writings,
they are not missionaries at all. The nameless group of the
twelve is accorded a christophany (1 Cor. 15:5). In Q, they
are twelve anonymous eschatological judge-figures. Would the
earliest material have portrayed them so diversely if Jesus
had appointed them as missionaries? It is of course true that
the apocryphal Acts are agreed in their portrayal of the twelve
as distinguished missionary pioneers. But who would regard
their late portrayal as reliable historical information filling
a lacuna in our knowledge of their original performance? Who
would claim that the grand reports about their alleged world-
wide travels are based on solid historical evidence? The historical role of the twelve is indeed shrouded in secrecy, and

in view of this R. Fuller's advice to relegate the whole historical question into the background is at least understandable. "Whether or not the twelve already existed prior to the crucifixion," he says nonchalantly, "need not . . . concern us."[131] Understandable though this view may be, it still does not settle the question. Why should it not concern us?

In conclusion, the appearance of the twelve in three independent strands of the early Christian tradition attests to the high pre-synoptic age of the Christian twelve concept.[132] However, the disparate function played by the twelve in these early materials, along with their mysterious disappearance even before the start of the earliest Christian mission,[133] does not suggest their appointment by the earthly Jesus.[134] The creation of the Christian twelve concept thus falls into the earliest post-Easter period of the Christian community, and it should not be difficult to determine the religious motifs which gave birth to this concept. The rationale behind the Christian twelve concept will occupy us in the following section of our study.

1. W. Schmithals, <u>The Office of Apostle in the Early Church</u>
   (Nashville: Abingdon, 1969), 275.

2. K. Aland (ed.), <u>Vollständige Konkordanz zum Griechischen</u>
   <u>Neuen Testament</u> (Berlin/New York: Walter de Gruyter,
   1975), 86. The textual variant (Hesychian text, etc.) to
   Luke 9:1 (E. Nestle ed. , <u>Novum Testamentum Graece</u>, 26th
   Edition) has been omitted from the list.

3. J. Knox, <u>Marcion and the New Testament: An Essay in the</u>
   <u>Early History of the Canon</u> (Chicago: University of Chicago Press, 1942), 128f; G. Klein, <u>Die Zwölf Apostel:</u>
   <u>Ursprung und Gestalt einer Idee</u> (Göttingen: Vandenhoeck,
   1961), 189-192.

4. K. Aland (ed.), <u>Vollständige Konkordanz zum Griechischen</u>
   <u>Neuen Testament</u> (Berlin: W. de Gruyter, 1975), 86. Acts
   14:4.14 do not speak of the <u>twelve</u> apostles.

5. Acts 1:21-22.

6. Acts 13:31.

7. Acts 10:41.

8. Acts 1:16.

9. H. Conzelmann, "Luke's Place in the Development of Early
   Christianity," <u>Studies in Luke-Acts</u> (ed. by Leander E.
   Keck/J. L. Martyn) (Nashville: Abingdon Press, 1966),
   298-316, 306.

10. K. Lake, "The Twelve and the Apostles," Note VI in <u>The</u>
    <u>Beginnings of Christianity</u>, Part I, <u>The Acts of the</u>
    <u>Apostles</u>, ed. by Foakes Jackson/K. Lake, Vol. V, with
    additional notes, etc. ed. by K. Lake/H. J. Cadbury
    (London: Macmillan, 1933), 37-59, 40.

11. Cf. C. K. Barrett, <u>Luke the Historian in Recent Study</u>
    (London: Epworth Press, 1961), 12-19, 49-50.

12. W. Schmithals, <u>The Office of Apostle in The Early Church</u>,
    277.

13. Ibid., 264.

14. Cf. Charles H. Talbert, <u>Luke and the Gnostics: An Exami-</u>
    <u>nation of the Lucan Purpose</u> (Nashville: Abingdon Press,
    1966), 54, fn. 12.

15. A. Ehrhardt, The Apostolic Succession in the First Two
    Centuries of the Church (London: Lutterworth Press,
    1953), 59.

16. G. Klein, Die Zwölf Apostel: Ursprung und Gestalt einer
    Idee, 202-216. In comparison with Mk. 1:16-20, the eye-
    witness passages of Lk. 1:2 and Acts 1:21f. represent
    late theological concepts (E. Haenchen, Der Weg Jesu.
    Eine Erklärung des Markusevangeliums und der Kanonischen
    Parallelen [Berlin: Töpelmann, 1966], 39). This leads
    Charles H. Talbert to state that "the concept of the
    closed group of the twelve ruling the church is due to
    the Lucan hand" (Luke and the Gnostics, 85).

17. W. Schmithals, The Office of Apostle in the Early Church,
    268.277.

18. J. Munck, "Paul, the Apostles, and the Twelve," Studia
    Theologica Cura Ordinum Theologorum Scandinavicorum,
    Vol. III, Fasc. I-II (1949), 96-110, 108.

19. It must be noted that Luke transformed Paul into a faith-
    ful subordinate of Jerusalem decades after his death
    (Acts 20:25.38; 27:24). Cf. H. O. Guenther, "The Nega-
    tive Fascination of New Testament Language with Judaism,"
    Shingaku-Kenkyu, Theological Studies: Kwansei Gakuin,
    Vol. 31 (1983), 23-75, especially 52-62.

20. Cf. J. Knox, Marcion and the New Testament, 120.123.
    128.130f.; G. Klein, Die Zwölf Apostel, 111-113.

21. The following quotations (footnotes 21-40) are taken from
    The Apostolic Fathers, The Loeb Classical Library. Engl.
    Translation by K. Lake, 2 Vols., Vol. I (London: W. Heine-
    mann Ltd., 1912, repr. 1965). Ign. to Eph. 9:1; 16:1,
    Ign. to Phil. 7:2, 8:1.

22. Ign. to Eph. 6:1.

23. Ign. to Trall. 2:1.

24. Ign. to Eph. 17:1.

25. Ign. to Eph. 11:2.

26. Ign. to Magn. 3:1.

27. Ign. to Trall. 3:1, 7:1, 12:2; Ign. to Eph. 11:2; Ign. to
    Magn. 7:1; 13:1-2; Ign. to Phil. 5:1; Ign. to Smyr. 8:1.

28. W. Schmithals, The Office of Apostle in the Early Church,
    240.

29. Ign. to Polyc. 8:1.

30. Ign. to Polyc. 7:2.

31. Ign. to Rom. 4:3; Ign. to Smyr. 11:1 suggests that the
     bishop of Antioch was familiar with Paul's letters.

32. I Clemens, 42:1f.

33. Cf. 1 Clemens, 5:3-5.

34. Polycarp to Phil. 3:1-2; 7:2; 8:1; 11:2.

35. Polyc. to Phil. 6:3.

36. Polyc. to Phil. 9:1.

37. Didache 11:3.

38. Didache 11:4.

39. Didache 11:5.

40. Didache 11:5-6.

41. K. Lake, "The Twelve and the Apostles," 51.

42. D. Flusser, "The Pesher of Isaiah and the Twelve Apos-
     tles," E. L. Sukenik Memorial Volume, Eretz-Israel,
     Vol. 8 (Jerusalem: Israel Exploration Society, 1967),
     52-62. The full translation of the Hebrew pesher is
     found in J. M. Baumgarten, "The Duodecimal Courts of
     Qumran, Revelation and the Sanhedrin," Journal of Bibli-
     cal Literature, Vol. 95 (1976), 59-78. With the signif-
     icance of the pesher we will deal later in our study.
     It is worth noting here that the fourth gospel does not
     mention the twelve at all. In John's gospel, the empha-
     sis is on the believer's immediate encounter with the
     Revealer. "This is the background against which we must
     interpret the absence of any conception of an ecclesi-
     astically privileged ministry, an absence which shows up
     most clearly in the lack of any emphasis on the aposto-
     late and in the way in which the apostles cede pride of
     place to the 'beloved disciple'." (E. Käsemann, "The
     Structure and Purpose of the Prologue to John's Gospel,"
     New Testament Questions of Today, tr. by W. J. Montague
     [London: SCM Press, 1969], 138-167, 162).

43. Barnabas 8:3; 5:9.

44. G. Klein calls Luke an advocate of the apostolic "numerus
     clausus" (Die Zwölf Apostel, 112).

45. Ignatius, Clemens, Polycarp and the Book of Revelation
     speak of past apostles. Didache refers to current apos-
     tles.

46. Cf. Letter of Barnabas. W. Schmithals' comment that the
apostolic fathers represent the "unreflective thought of
the Christian community . . . down to the present day"
(The Office of Apostle in the Early Church, 279) is
right to the point. "Without distinction of rank,"
Schmithals says, "the twelve and Paul, the disciples of
the historical Jesus and the disciples of the exalted
Christ, qualify as apostles . . ." (ibid. 279f.). The
observation that the typical marks of early Catholicism
(i.e., references to the institutional understanding of
the church and its offices; the emphasis on apostolic
succession; unequivocal statements highlighting the
church's defensive attitudes to the threat of gnosti-
cizing tendencies, etc.) are absent from Luke's two
compositions can hardly be used to contest the affinity
between Luke's Acts and the writings of Justin Martyr.
By dating Acts between 70-90 C.E., H. Conzelmann (contra J. Knox) tries to separate the first Church History
(Acts) chronologically from Justin Martyr by more than
fifty years. Since Luke wrote a history of the apostolic
church, he could not afford to project the theology of
early Catholicism in its entirety into the apostolic age
but had to be satisfied with introducing what H. Conzelmann himself rightly calls "tendencies" leading to this
theology (H. Conzelmann, "Luke's Place in the Development of Early Christianity," 304-309).

47. W. Schmithals, The Office of Apostle in the Early Church,
277.

48. Lk. 1:2; Acts 1:21f.; 10:41; 13:31.

49. In his review of Luke-Acts in recent study, C. K. Barrett
points out that Luke is the only writer "who makes any
conscious attempt to show how, when the earthly life of
Jesus was over, the Church came into being, and to relate
the one to the other" (Luke the Historian in Recent Study,
55). Luke's strong dislike for 'new' and, as he undoubtedly believed, 'perverse' teachings shows through in
Lk. 5:39 and in Acts 20:29f. For a further discussion of
these tendencies see H. O. Guenther, "The Negative Fascination of the New Testament Language with Judaism," Shingaku Kenkyu, 52-62. C. K. Barrett sees both Luke and
John deal with the two chief problems of the outgoing
first century, i.e., gnosticism and eschatology (Luke the
Historian in Recent Study, 62).

50. E. Best, The Temptation and the Passion: The Markan So-
teriology (Cambridge: At the University Press, 1965), 178.

51. K. Lake rightly notes that Mark nowhere made the suggestion "that Jesus contemplated the foundation of a
'Church'," ("The Twelve and the Apostles," 47; cf. also
39). W. H. Kelber's assumption that the three disciples,

Peter, James and John, mentioned repeatedly in Mark's gospel (Mk. 5:37; 9:2; 14:33), were "representatives of the twelve" ("The Hour of the Son of Man and the Temptation of the Disciples," in The Passion in Mark. Studies on Mark 14-16, ed. by W. H. Kelber [Philadelphia: Fortress Press, 1976], 41-60, 58) is textually unfounded. There is no room in Mark's gospel for any 'representation of the twelve'. As W. H. Kelber himself rightly observes, the twelve (including the three) are throughout "negative models of discipleship" (W. H. Kelber, "From Passion Narrative to Gospel," The Passion in Mark. Studies on Mark 14-16, 153-180, 174). Even E. Best goes too far when he infers from Mk. 3:13-19 that "though Mark may not give to 'apostle' a technical sense, we cannot deny that in the appointment of the Twelve there are the rudiments of organisation" (The Temptation and the Passion, 117). This may be true for Luke's reading of Mark's mind, not for Mark himself. As Mk. 13:3 demonstrates, Mark could very readily add a fourth member to the group of the three. The three are for Mark Jesus' most intimate followers but not the representatives of the twelve!

52. Mk. 11:14/11:11; 14:12.14/14:17; 9:31a/9:35a. Cf. also E. Best, "Mark's Use of the Twelve," Zeitschrift für die Neutestamentliche Wissenschaft, Vol. 69 (1978), 11-35, 32.

53. Mk. 3:14.

54. E. Best, The Temptation and the Passion, 187.

55. G. Theissen, The First Followers of Jesus. A Sociological Analysis of the Earliest Christianity (London: SCM Press, 1978), 9.

56. R. Bultmann, The History of the Synoptic Tradition, tr. by J. Marsh (New York: Harper, 2nd ed. 1968), 62.

57. Mk. 4:10; 6:7; 9:35a; 10:32; 11:11; 14:17.

58. R. Bultmann, The History of the Synoptic Tradition, 345. The strained σὺν τοῖς δώδεκα (Mk. 4:10) may well stem from the hand of a copyist. Mark found the motif for the appointment of the twelve, as R. Bultmann suggests, "in their continuing in company with Jesus . . . as in their being sent out . . ." (ibid. 341).

59. The pre-Markan pronouncement story of Mk. 1:16f. knows nothing of the twelve. The references to the 'three disciples' (Mk. 5:37; 9:2; 14:33) and to 'the four' (13: 3) do not suggest knowledge of the twelve either. Mk. 10: 41 refers to 'the ten', with a side-reading of D: οἱ λοιποί.

60. E. Best, "Mark's Use of the Twelve," 11-35.

61. Ibid. 32.

62. Ibid. 34.

63. Ibid.

64. Ibid.; cf. 15.

65. Ibid. 15.

66. Ibid. 21.

67. Ibid. 25.

68. Ibid. 29.

69. Ibid.

70. E. Käsemann, "The Disciples of John the Baptist in Ephesus," Essays on New Testament Themes, Studies in Biblical Theology, tr. by W. J. Montague (London: SCM Press, 1964), 136-148.

71. J. Knox, Marcion and the New Testament, 118.

72. E. Best, "Mark's Use of the Twelve," 35.

73. K. Lake, "The Twelve and the Apostles," 47.

74. No sharp distinction exists in Matthew's gospel between the disciples (οἱ μαθηταί) and the twelve (οἱ δώδεκα). Cf. Mk. 4:10/Mt. 13:10; Mk. 6:7/Mt. 10:1; Mk. 9:35/Mt. 18:1, etc. "Matthew tempers the traditional view of Peter in order to enhance the prominence of all of the disciples" (J. D. Kingsbury, "The Figure of Peter in Matthew's Gospel as a Theological Problem," Journal for Bibl. Literature 98 [1979], 67-83, 74).

75. G. Bornkamm, "End-Expectation and Church in Matthew," Tradition and Interpretation in Matthew, ed. by G. Bornkamm et al., tr. by P. Scott (London: SCM Press, 1963), 43. Cf. Mt. 13:16.23.51; 14:33; 16:12; 17:13; 26:2.

76. More on the basis of common sense than through exegetical analyses, K. Lake ("The Twelve and the Apostles") noted that the designation οἱ ἀπόστολοι (Mk. 6:30) is "a description rather than a 'title'" (46). This observation has been affirmed by the more subtle studies of the literary critics. It is true that within the context of the second gospel Mk. 6:30 most probably refers to the twelve. However, redaction-critically the verse is in its entirety a transitional passage of Markan origin, designed to relate the feeding story (Mk. 6:32-44) to the pre-Markan

pericope about the commissioning of the twelve (Mk. 6:
6b-13), as R. Bultmann (The History of the Synoptic
Tradition, 244.340) rightly observed. Norman R. Petersen (Literary Criticism for New Testament Critics [Phila-
delphia: Fortress Press, 1978], 56) expanded Bultmann's
view by suggesting that the relationship between the commission of Mk. 3:14f. and Mk.6:(6b).7f.is a 'literary
creation' of Mark. In the same vein, E. Best (The Temptation and the Passion, 187) designated Mk. 6:7.12f.30
as Markan literary creations.

77. As the side-readings to Mk. 3:14-16 demonstrate, the tex-
     tual situation is quite unclear. The reference to οὕς καὶ
     ἀπόστολοι ὠνόμασεν is well attested by the Alexandrian and
     the Eastern texts (B, אּ , C?,ϑ ,φ , sa, bo, sy[hmg]). Re-
     fusing to confuse the attempt to establish the most au-
     thentic Markan text with the question concerning the
     historicity of the twelve and their later position in the
     church, E. Haenchen holds it possible that 'Luke may have
     derived Lk. 6:13 from Mk. 3:14" (Der Weg Jesu, 139). On
     the other hand, some manuscripts do not contain the refer-
     ence at all (C[2], K, A, D, 0133, λ, lat, syr[s.p.] etc.). The
     redundancy of ἀπόστολοι / ἀποστέλλειν (Mk. 3:14), plus the
     importance which Luke, in contrast to Mark (cf. Mk. 6:35/
     Lk. 9:12; Mk. 14:17/Lk. 22:14), attributed to the twelve
     apostles, strongly suggests that the later copyists, in-
     terested in and familiar with the church's twelve-apostle
     institution, inserted the Lukan reference into the Markan
     text. In the fifth century, the institution was taken
     for granted, so that the copyists could not afford to even
     out the style of the passage and to omit the redundant
     reference to οὕς καὶ ἀπόστολοι ὠνόμασεν, which had not
     been in the Syriac text in the first place. Ch. H. Tal-
     bert's suggestion that Luke himself added the reference
     must be taken seriously. "This . . . is in the interest
     of his motif" (Luke and the Gnostics, 23). Even E. Haen-
     chen admits that Mark had no unique function for the
     'apostles' whom he regards as having been in the original
     text. G. Strecker (Der Weg der Gerechtigkeit. Unter-
     suchung zur Theologie des Matthäus [Göttingen: Vandenhoek
     & Ruprecht, 3rd ed., 1971], 194) points out that Mt. 10:
     2-4 contains several 'modifying additions' ('erläuternde
     Zusätze"). It is thus no longer possible to argue back
     from Matthew's text to Mark's.

78. Instead of τῶν δὲ δώδεκα ἀποστόλων, the Sinai-Syriac reads
     τῶν δὲ δώδεκα μαθητῶν. The reading is still not strong
     enough to suggest authenticity.

79. C. D. Kilpatrick, The Origins of the Gospel according to
     St. Matthew (Oxford: At the Clarendon Press, 1946), 126.

80. Siegfried Schulz, Q: Die Spruchquelle der Evangelisten
     (Zürich: Theologischer Verlag, 1972), 414; cf. 336.

81. The Q hypothesis--for R. H. Streeter still "short of
     certainty" (B. H. Streeter, The Four Gospels, A Study of
     Origins [London: Macmillan, 1924], 184)--represents in
     H. J. Holtzmann's judgment "the most probable solution
     of the synoptic problem" (H. J. Holtzmann, Lehrbuch der
     Historisch - Kritischen Einleitung in das Neue Testa-
     ment [Freiburg i.B.: J.C.B. Mohr (P. Siebeck), 3. Aufl.,
     1892], 366). Although still rejected by some (A. Farrer,
     "On dispensing with Q," in Studies in the Gospels, ed. by
     D. E. Nineham [Oxford: Blackwell, 1955]; W. R. Farmer,
     The Synoptic Problem [New York: Macmillan, 1964]), the Q
     hypothesis is today generally accepted by most New Testa-
     ment scholars. The verbal agreements between the Matthean
     and Lukan materials convinced A.v. Harnack (New Testament
     Studies II. The Sayings of Jesus [London: Williams & Nor-
     gate and New York: G. P. Putnam's Sons, 1908])--who was
     initially sceptical of the Q hypothesis (40)--of the
     validity of the Q solution. Q is for Harnack "a price-
     less compilation of the sayings of Jesus" (249), a hetero-
     geneous document "without any clearly discernible bias,
     whether apologetic, didactic, ecclesiastical, national,
     or anti-national" (171). M. Dibelius (From Tradition to
     Gospel, tr. by B. L. Woolf [New York: Ch. Scribner's Sons,
     1935]), taking issue with Harnack's designation of Q as a
     'document', called Q "a stratum" rather than a full-
     fledged source (235). In Dibelius' view, the sayings were
     laced together "for a hortatory end" (246), i.e., for
     practical purposes (262), with no discernible narrative or
     overall theological intent. Modern scholarship has suc-
     ceeded in further clarifying the character of Q. For H.
     Tödt (The Son of Man in the Synoptic Tradition, tr. by
     D. M. Barton [Philadelphia: Westminster, 1965]), the post-
     Easter Q community continued Jesus' pre-Easter proclama-
     tion of God's imminent reign (249). A thoroughgoing anal-
     ysis of the literary forms of the Q texts led S. Schulz
     (Q: Die Spruchquelle der Evangelisten) to distinguish be-
     tween older (Palestinian-Jewish-Christian) and younger
     (Hellenistic-Jewish-Christian) layers of Q. D. Lührmann
     (Die Redaktion der Logienquelle [Neukirchen: Neukirchener
     Verlag, 1969]), even tried to identify the theology of the
     Q editor (redactor) (8). Lührmann demonstrates that the
     Q redaction shows through in the way in which the redactor
     collected his material (84). The emphasis on God's judg-
     ment over Israel is, in Lührmann's perspective, the redac-
     tor's overall theological orientation. There is no con-
     sensus of opinion with regard to D. Lührmann's method and
     his conclusions. Both R. A. Edwards (A Theology of Q
     [Philadelphia: Fortress Press, 1976], 24.78), and P.
     Hoffmann (Studien zur Theologie der Logienquelle, Münster:
     Aschendorff, 1972 , 332) have affirmed the apocalyptic-

eschatological tendencies of Q. By contrast and following
the lead of J. M. Robinson et al., A. D. Jacobson has persuasively argued that the organizing principle of Q at the
compositional stage was Wisdom as the sender of prophets
(Wisdom Christology in Q, Claremont Graduate School, Ph.D.
Dissertation [University Microfilms International, 1978],
228).

82. Lk. 10:2-12/Mt. 9:37f.; 10:7b-16.

83. S. Schulz, Q: Die Spruchquelle der Evangelisten, 404f.
The Source speaks of ἐργάται (mercenarii), not of δοῦλοι
(slaves), nor of γεωργοί (tenants).

84. K. H. Rengstorf, "ἀποστέλλειν etc.," Theological Dictionary of the New Testament, ed. by G. Kittel and tr.
by G. W. Bromiley, Vol. I (Grand Rapids: Wm. B. Eerdmans,
1964), 398. 400. 404. K. H. Rengstorf assumes that the
Jewish   שליח -institution is "the closest parallel to
the New Testament ἀπόστολος " (ibid. 414). W. Schmithals
(The Office of Apostle in the Early Church, 110), G.
Klein (Die Zwölf Apostel, 26-38) and K. Lake ("The Twelve
and the Apostles," 49) have challenged this assumption
with valid reasons. A. Ehrhardt (The Apostolic Succession in the First Two Centuries of the Church, 16f.) is
critical of K. H. Rengstorf's conclusions but does not
reject them outright. C. K. Barrett ("Shaliah and
Apostle," Donum Gentilicium, New Testament Studies in
Honour of David Daube, ed. by E. Bammel/C. K. Barrett/
W. D. Davies [Oxford: Clarendon, 1978], 88-102) affirms
that the Jewish evidence for a   שליח -institution in
New Testament times is scanty (95). He also recognizes
the difference between the eschatological nature of the
Christian apostle and the legal   שליח -institution.
But he nonetheless uses the New Testament references to
apostleship (Paul's apostolate) to establish a link
(sic!) between the Christian ἀπόστολος, and the Jewish
שליח   (100f.). The fact that the LXX uses ἀποστέλλειν
700 times cannot be ignored. Rengstorf rightly observed that etymologically "the original meaning of
ἀποστέλλειν did not come to be restricted to the exclusive significance of the divine sending and authori-
zation of a man" (TDNT, 400). He is also aware of the
fact that in Josephus, John, and occasionally in Paul
(Rm. 8:3), ἀποστέλλειν and πέμπειν - πέμψαι are used
interchangeably. But Rengstorf nonetheless claims that
when πέμπειν (which occurs 26 times in the LXX) "is used
in the New Testament the emphasis is on the fact of
sending" (404). Ἀποστέλλειν, on the other hand, is used
to demonstrate "the commission linked with" the fact of
sending (ibid.). The interchangeability of the two
terms in biblical and non-biblical writings does not

support Rengstorf's claim that ἀποστέλλειν is exclusively a "technical term for the sending of a messenger with a special task" (ibid.). It is true, however, that in the New Testament ἀποστέλλειν is on the way to becoming "a theological term" (ibid. 406).

85. Lk. 10:2/Mt. 9:38; Lk. 10:16/Mt. 10:40; Lk. 7:27/Mt. 11: 10; Lk. 14:17/Mt. 22:3; Lk. 13:34/Mt. 23:37.

86. J. Weeden, Mark - Traditions in Conflict (Philadelphia: Fortress, 1971) 43; Cf. J. Held, "Matthew as Interpreter of Miracle Stories," Tradition and Interpretation in Matthew, 191.

87. The question as to whether or not Mark knew the Q Source (or at least some Q texts) does not seem to come to rest. In his essay "Der Einfluss der Logienquelle auf das Markusevangelium" (Zeitschrift für die Neutestamentliche Wissenschaft 70 [1979], 141-165), W. Schenk offers a new rendition of J. Wellhausen's claim that Mark had epitomized the Q Source, of which he had full knowledge (J. Wellhausen, Einleitung in die drei ersten Evangelien [Berlin: Reimer, 1905], 46). In doing so, W. Schenk questions the usefulness of the two-source hypothesis for the clarification of the relationship between Mark and Q. Intent on demonstrating "the influence of Q upon the Markan redaction" (141), Schenk focussed his attention on the approx. 30 odd sayings which appear in both Mark and Q. He argues that although the pre-Markan tradition is chronologically primary to Q (cf. W. Schenk, Synopse zur Redenquelle der Evangelien: Q-Synopse und Rekonstruktion in deutscher Übersetzung mit kurzen Erläuterungen [Düsseldorf: Patmos, 1981], 132-133), Mark nonetheless edited several pre-Markan sayings (Mk. 3:28f.; 8:12.38, for instance) and pre-Markan parables (Mk. 4: 31-32, for instance) by taking the Q rendition of these passages into account ("Der Einfluss der Logienquelle auf das Markusevangelium," 146.161). W. Schenk's recourse to rather speculative arguments does not commend his assumptions. Why, for instance, did Mark fail to edit the familiar Son of Man title into Mk. 3:28, if the Source was available to him? That Mark's interest in the historical Jesus and his concern for a "more developed" christology prompted the elimination of the title from the primary pre-Markan text (ibid. 148.162) is hardly a cogent argument. Likewise, Mark's failure to exhibit any knowledge of Q's wisdom traditions is not really explained by the speculative contention that the second evangelist may have been critically disposed towards Q's Sophia christology. A. D. Jacobson's definition that "Q is . . . that portion of Matthew not taken over by Mark but used by Luke" (Wisdom Christology in Q, 226) accommodates the

available data more adequately than W. Schenk's specula-
tive interpretations. For further discussion cf. A. D.
Jacobson, "The Literary Unity of Q," Journal of Biblical
Literature, 101 (1982), 365-389, 373, fn. 30.

88. Cf. H. O. Guenther, "The Negative Fascination of the New
Testament Language with Judaism," Shingaku Kenkyu, 36f.

89. S. Schulz, Q: Die Spruchquelle der Evangelisten, 336;
O. H. Steck, Israel und das gewaltsame Geschick der
Propheten. Untersuchungen zur Überlieferung des
deuteronomistischen Geschichtsbildes im Alten Testa-
ment, Spätjudentum und Urchristentum (Neukirchen-Vluyn,
Neukirchener Verlag, 1967), 29f.; against A. v. Harnack
The Sayings of Jesus, 98f.; 103f.; 139 and E. Haenchen
"Matthäus 23" in Gott und Mensch. Gesammelte Aufsätze
(Tübingen: J. C. B. Mohr [P. Siebeck]), 1965, 29-54, 44.

90. S. Schulz, Q: Die Spruchquelle der Evangelisten, 336.

91. These differences relate to both the disciples' names
and the sequence in which these names are listed.

92. Mk. 3:16-19; Mt. 10:2-4; Lk. 6:14-16; Acts 1:13.

93. R. Bultmann, The History of the Synoptic Tradition, 345.

94. Cf. E. Bammel, "Herkunft und Funktion der Traditionselemente in 1 Kor. 15:1-11," Theologische Zeitschrift
11 (1955), 401-419, 406.

95. Aside from A. v. Harnack's attempt to psychologize the
texts by converting Peter's allegedly pre-Easter vision
of Jesus on the mountain of transfiguration into a point
of departure for all later (post-Easter) appearances to
individuals and groups of witnesses ("Die Verklärungsgeschichte Jesu, der Bericht des Paulus (1 Kor. 15:3f)
und die beiden Christus-Visionen des Petrus," Sitzungsberichte der Preussischen Akademie der Wissenschaften
[Berlin, 1922],62-80), his division of the pre-Pauline
formula of 1 Cor. 15:3f into two major parts has been
accepted by a number of scholars.   According to
Harnack, the early formula reached from v.3 (ὅτι Χριστὸς
ἀπέθανεν) to v. 5 (ὅτι ὤφθη Κηφᾷ, εἶτα τοῖς δώδεκα).
For Harnack, the two appearances (v.5) took place in
Galilee. The change from the formulistic ὅτι-εἶτα-
clause (v.5) to the narrative ἔπειτα ὤφθη (vv.6-7) marks
the join between the earliest formula (vv.3-5) and the
later additions to it (vv.6f). Harnack holds that the
appearances listed in the later part occurred in Jerusalem. He seems to follow here the lead of K. Holl ("Der
Kirchenbegriff des Paulus in seinem Verhältnis zu dem

der Urgemeinde: 1921," <u>Gesammelte Aufsätze zur Kirchen-</u>
<u>geschichte</u>, Bd. 11: Der Osten [Darmstadt: Wissenschaft-
liche Buchgesellschaft, 1964]) who located the appearances to Cephas and the twelve in Galilee, while claiming that the appearance to the five hundred brethren
occurred in Jerusalem (46f.). According to K. Holl, the
appearance to the ἀποστόλοις πᾶσιν did not happen to
"a larger circle of full-time missionaries" (47), as
J. B. Lightfoot had claimed it (<u>Saint Paul's Epistle to</u>
<u>the Galatians</u>, rev. text, 8th ed. [London: MacMillan,
1884], 93f.). It rather was an all-inclusive and final
one, experienced by 'all apostles' (i.e., the twelve and
James) (48.50). The appearance to James highlights, says
Holl, the position held by him in the Jerusalem church
(Gal. 2:9) (50). The conclusive nature of the appearance to 'all apostles' is clear from the fact that Paul
called himself an ἔκτρωμα, an exception (50). G. Lüdemann ("Zum Antipaulinismus im frühen Christentum,"
<u>EvTheologie</u> 40 (1980), 437-455) agrees with Harnack's
delimitation of the early formula (451). E. Bammel
("Herkunft und Funktion der Traditionselemente in 1 Kor.
15: 1-11,") divides the formula into three parts:
1. Χριστὸς ἀπέθανεν . . . καὶ ὤφθη, partly in agreement
with Harnack; 2. ὤφθη Κηφᾷ . . . πεντακοσίοις ἀδελφοῖς
ἐφάπαξ; 3. ὤφθη Ἰακώβῳ . . . ἀποστόλοις πᾶσιν. He
holds that the three parts show a considerable development in the church's christology. They also mirror
leadership struggles fought in the Jerusalem church between 40-45 C.E. While for Harnack οἱ δώδεκα (v.5) and
οἱ ἀπόστολοι πάντες (v.7) signify the same group (<u>op.</u>
<u>cit</u>. 66.68), E. Bammel, following K. Holl, stresses the
all-inclusive nature of the οἱ ἀπόστολοι πάντες, with
James and the twelve being part of them. Charles H.
Talbert suggests an even wider group than the twelve
(<u>Luke and the Gnostics</u>, 85). E. Bammel's view that the
early claims to an appearance constituted claims to early
church leadership is worth considering. The listing of
groups is in keeping with the late Jewish <u>Zeugenrecht</u>
(rules of evidence). The testimony of individual witnesses (Cephas, Paul) would have been inconclusive (E.
Bammel, "Herkunft und Funktion der Traditionselemente in
1 Kor. 15:1-11," 406.415). An appearance of the Lord was
thought to be legally valid only if it had been a group
testimony (<u>ibid</u>. 415). The Damascus Rule of Qumran
affirms the standing practice of Judaism: <u>Unus testis</u>
<u>nullus testis</u> (G. Vermes, <u>The Dead Sea Scrolls</u>. <u>Qumran</u>
<u>in Perspective</u> [London: Collins, 1977], 100f.). Paul
neutralized, argues E. Bammel, the church's political
intentions of the original formulations by transposing
the formula into the key of christology. All the appearances now ascertain with one voice that 'The Lord appeared
to the Household of God' (<u>op. cit</u>., 416). In line with

this general discussion, R. H. Fuller (The Formation of the Resurrection Narratives [New York: Macmillan, 1971]) suggests "three separate informants" for the early formula (28). Paul's interest in the consolidation of the church made him collect these accounts during his first Jerusalem visit (ibid.). The Lord's appearances to Cephas and to the twelve thus have, says Fuller, church-founding significance (ibid. 35), while those to James and all the apostles inaugurated the church's Gentile mission (ibid. 38.49). J. Munck ("Paul, the Apostles, and the Twelve") does not think that any of the names mentioned in the formula were part of the pre-Pauline creed. "Very possibly," says Munck, "it is the last name in the list of witnesses -- Paul himself -- which has made it necessary for Paul to add the other names" (ibid. 105).

96. Without giving any evidence, K. Lake suggests that Paul may have known the twelve personally (K. Lake, "The Twelve and the Apostles," 40.).

97. A. Fridrichsen ("The Apostle and His Message," Uppsala Universitets Arsskrift 1947, 2-23, 18, fn. 12) rightly points out that the twelve must not be confused with the πρὸ ἐμοῦ ἀπόστολοι of Gal. 1:17. The latter were still known to Paul. E. Haenchen does not confuse the two groups. He still insists on the historicity of the twelve (Der Weg Jesu, 138), though without offering any substantiation.

98. G. Heinrici, Kritisch-exegetisches Handbuch über den ersten Brief an die Korinther (1881), 400 (quoted by E. Bammel in "Herkunft und Funktion der Traditionselemente in 1 Kor. 15:1-11," 405).

99. D, G, vul, sy[h] write 'he appeared to the eleven'. This shows that the copyists had noticed the incongruity between the Lord's visitation to the twelve (1 Cor. 15:5) and the risen Lord's appearance to the eleven (Acts 1:3, 6-17).

100. G. Theissen draws attention to the fact that the structural homologue for the saying is provided by the way in which the Son of Man was expected to judge Israel (The First Followers of Jesus, 27).

101. Most likely Luke removed the Q numeral (δώδεκα) in order to avoid any allusion to Judas' possible participation in the divine judgment. Judas was apparently not part of the Q twelve, which makes them into a post-Easter group different from the pre-Markan twelve.

102. Matthew inserted the saying into the story about the Rich
      Young Man (Mt. 19:16-30). Peter's response to Jesus
      (Mt. 19:27: "we have left everything") implies that the
      twelve disciples (αὐτοῖς 19:28) were for Matthew the
      bearers of the promise (Mt. 19:28: ὑμεῖς). Can it be
      presupposed that the isolated Q saying itself was also
      addressed to the twelve disciples? Luke did not work the
      saying into the Rich Young Man pericope (which is earlier
      in Lk; cf. Lk. 18:18-30). It rather appears within the
      passion narrative, in the context of the question concern-
      ing the disciples' rank (cf. Mk. 10:41-45). The ὑμεῖς
      of the original Q saying are for Luke the twelve disciples
      (in Luke's theology the 'twelve apostles'). In both cases
      it is the context which determines the identity of ὑμεῖς.
      Ambivalence in the identity of subjects is also found out-
      side the New Testament literature. In Qumran's Community
      Rule, for instance, the Guardian and the Interpreter of
      the Law represent the same person. In the Damascus Rule,
      "the Levite and the guardian were one and the same per-
      son" (G. Vermes, The Dead Sea Scrolls in English [Balti-
      more, Md.: Penguin Books, 1962, repr. 1965], 25).

103. Ὑμεῖς καθήσεσθε ἐπὶ θρόν(ων) τὰς δώδεκα φύλας κρίνοντες
      τοῦ Ἰσραήλ (you will sit on thrones judging the twelve
      tribes of Israel). Can it really be said that this is a
      "small amount of common material" (R. A. Edwards, A The-
      ology of Q, 145)? S. Schulz assigns Lk. 22:28-30/Mt. 19:
      28 to Q (Q: Die Spruchquelle der Evangelisten, 330), in
      agreement with D. Lührmann (Die Redaktion der Logienquelle,
      109f.; most probably 75.90), and P. Hoffmann (Studien zur
      Theologie der Logienquelle, 5.42.150.304). A Polag regards
      the passage as a probable Q text (Die Christologie der
      Logienquelle [Neukirchen-Vluyn: Neukirchener Verlag, 1977],
      6) but still expresses a modicum of doubt: "wenn das logion
      zu Q gehörte und den Abschluss bildete . . ." (11). W.
      Schenk lists the passage as the closing part of the Source
      (Synopse zur Redenquelle der Evangelien, 130).

104. 1) Mt.: οἱ ἀκολουθήσαντες; Lk.: οἱ διαμεμενηκότες
      ("you who have followed me"/"you who have persisted with
      me"). 2) Mt.: ἐν τῇ παλιγγενεσίᾳ ("in the new world"
      which is for G. Strecker 'the parousia,' G. Strecker,
      Der Weg der Gerechtigkeit, 238); Lk.: ἐν τῇ βασιλείᾳ
      ("in the kingdom"). In Strecker's view, these terms
      derive from the Hellenistic tradition (ibid. 238, fn. 3).
      Would Matthew have omitted his favourite term βασιλεία
      if it had been in his version of Q? It is noteworthy
      that παλιγγενεσία is an important term in the Hermetic
      literature (W. C. Grese, Corpus Hermeticum XIII and
      Early Christian Literature, in Studia and Corpus Her-
      meticum Novi Testamenti, Vol. 5 [Leiden: E. J. Brill,
      1979], 2).

105. H. Tödt, The Son of Man in the Synoptic Tradition, 62f.;
     S. Schulz, Q: Die Spruchquelle der Evangelisten, 330-
     336. Schulz assigns the saying to the Hellenistic-
     Jewish strata of Q. D. Lührmann, Die Redaktion der
     Logienquelle, 75.90.109-110; P. Hoffmann, Studien zur
     Theologie der Logienquelle, 5.42.150.304; R. A.
     Edwards, A Theology of Q, xiii.51; H.C. Kee, Jesus in
     History: An Approach to the Study of the Gospels (New
     York: Harcourt, 1970) 70.72; B. H. Streeter's interest
     in the four source hypothesis (The Four Gospels) made
     him downplay the undeniable common elements in the
     saying by stating that "there are no points of contact
     between the parallels" of Mt. 19:28/Lk. 22:28-30 (sic!)
     (ibid. 288). Cf. fn. 103.104.

106. CD X (G. Vermes, The Dead Sea Scrolls in English, 111),
     Cf. H. Guenther, "The Negative Fascination of New Testa-
     ment Language with Judaism," Shingaku Kenkyu, 32-40.

107. H. J. Holtzmann assumes that the promise to judge the
     tribes of Israel was given "to all apostles" in their
     capacity as leaders (Die Synoptischen Evangelien: Ihr
     Ursprung und Geschichtlicher Charakter [Leipzig: W.
     Engelmann, 1863], 147). J. Wellhausen (Einleitung in
     die drei ersten Evangelien, 84) and recently S. Schulz
     (Q: Die Spruchquelle der Evangelisten, 335) follow
     Holtzmann's judgment in so far as they regard them as
     specifically chosen individuals. K. Lake indicates, on
     the one hand, that the promise was made to twelve indi-
     vidual disciples, but he also says, on the other hand,
     that Jesus addressed "the disciples" in general ("The
     Twelve and the Apostles," 37). H. Tödt (The Son of Man
     in the Synoptic Tradition) holds that in the earliest
     version -- which for him is Lk. 22:28-30 -- the promise
     was made "to all disciples who stayed with him," i.e.,
     with Jesus (64, cf. 255). W. Schenk does not think of
     individuals. He sees the saying addressed to all dis-
     ciples, the readers of the gospel being included:
     "Discipleship as faithfulness on the way stands under
     a promise which is to be affirmed in the future but is
     initiated by the Son of Man" (Synopse zur Redenquelle
     der Evangelien, 130).

108. Cf. footnote 102.

109. Throne: Dan. 7:22; Wisd. of Sol. 3:8; 1 En. 45:3; 61:8;
     62:2; 69:27; 108:12b; Judges: Wisd. of Sol. 3:8; To
     reign with Him: Dan. 7:22; 1 En. 1:9f; 94ff; 1QpHab
     5:4f. The judgment function, originally carried out by
     God himself or some patron angel, is in some writings
     already transferred to human agencies. In Dt. 32:8,
     for instance, the 'sons of God' are no longer members
     of God's heavenly council (so Ps. 82) but signify Israel

as a whole, or the elders of Israel. This process of
'humanizing' the celestial world is also discernible in
Isa. 24:21-23 where 'the host of heaven' is said to have
been thrown into the pit, while 'God's elders' are
praised for manifesting the divine glory (v.23). According to the midrashim, the elders are even promised to
judge the nations (Tanhuma Shemot 29; Wisd. of Sol.
3:7-8). "In Mt. 19:28 the concept of heavenly tribunal
emerges in a form which in substance is similar to that
found in the . . . midrashim" (J. M. Baumgarten, "The
Duodecimal Courts of Qumran, Revelation and the Sanhedrin," 70). It is true that in the midrashim, God himself still presides as judge over the nations (Gentiles).
In Mt. 19:28, it is the Son of Man who judges the tribes
of Israel. The shift, however, from God to his elect
(1 En.), to Melchizedek (11Q Melch 9) or the twelve (Q)
occurs already in the Jewish tradition.

110. Cf. footnote 87.

111. G. Strecker, Der Weg der Gerechtigkeit, 193f.

112. Cf. H. Tödt, The Son of Man in the Synoptic Tradition, 63.

113. K. Lake, "The Twelve and the Apostles," 37.39.47.

114. "Die Zwölfe, die nach der Auferstehung sich zusammen-
fanden, (waren) in der Hauptsache dieselben, wie die-
jenigen, die zu Lebzeiten Jesu ihn als der engere Kreis
begleiteten" (K. Holl, "Der Kirchenbegriff des Paulus in
seinem Verhältnis zu dem der Urgemeinde," 53, fn. 1).

115. K. Lake, "The Twelve and the Apostles," 41.

116. Ibid. 39. K. Lake rightly stresses that the disciples
were not "an official class in a new society," (ibid. 47)
nor were they "a closed corporation governing the Church"
(ibid. 58).

117. The reading of the gospels as history "wrongly supposes
that history or biography was the dominant optic of the
evangelist, and also that the evangelist could tell
whether the stories he included had a historical origin"
(Raymond E. Brown, The Birth of the Messiah. A Commentary on the Infancy Narratives in Matthew and Luke [New
York: Doubleday, 1977], 34).

118. J. Munck, "Paul, the Apostles, and the Twelve," 109. The
twelve-apostle institution is for Munck "a later trans-
ference of Paul's apostolate to the twelve disciples"
(ibid. 104).

119. *Ibid.* 108.

120. *Ibid.*

121. *Ibid.* 109.

122. M. Dibelius, Studies in the Acts of the Apostles, ed. by
     H. Greeven, tr. by Mary Ling (London: SCM Press, 1956),
     1-25; 102-108.

123. H. Conzelmann, History of Primitive Christianity, tr. by
     John E. Steely (Nashville: Abingdon, 1973), especially
     32.62.

124. E. Haenchen, The Acts of the Apostles: A Commentary,
     tr. by B. Noble et al. (Philadelphia: Westminster,
     1971), especially 81-110.

125. Charles H. Talbert, Luke and the Gnostics, 55-56.

126. For instance, the Pentecost account of Acts 2; Paul's
     five visits to Jerusalem (Acts 9:26; 11:30; 15:2;
     18:22 -- "he went up and greeted the [Jerusalem] church";
     21:15-17) (instead of three visits in the letters);
     the portrait of Paul, the subordinate of Jerusalem, etc.

127. Incidentally, Munck's suggestion of Luke's access to some
     otherwise unaccountable source materials about the twelve
     apostles is not the only area where this scholar prefers
     empty speculations to reasonable conjectures. His attempt
     to identify the synoptic pre-Easter with Paul's post-Easter
     twelve, who 'saw' the Lord (1 Cor. 15:5) (J. Munck,
     "Paul, the Apostles, and the Twelve," 105) is un-
     tenable. If Judas was one of the pre-Easter twelve, as
     J. Munck himself claims (ibid. 108), Jesus' betrayer
     should logically be excluded from the post-Easter group
     who had been accorded an appearance of the Lord. Scholars
     determined to prove the historicity of Jesus' call of the
     twelve often adduce arguments which undermine the stu-
     dent's trust in their historical judgments. They simply
     prove pre-conceived notions. "Pre-conceived notions are
     always the most serious obstacles to an exact knowledge
     of the past," says F. Cumont aptly (F. Cumont, The Ori-
     ental Religions in Roman Paganism [Chicago: Open Court
     Publ. Comp., 1911], Preface, xviii).

128. A. Polag, Die Christologie der Logienquelle, 24. fn.
     65.66.

129. J. Munck, "Paul, the Apostles, and the Twelve," 108.

130. Cf. footnote 96.

131. R. H. Fuller, The Formation of the Resurrection Narratives, 35.

132. We agree here with H. Tödt (The Son of Man in the Synoptic Tradition) who holds that "the concept of the twelve's representing the community of the last days, the Church as the true Israel, appears to have developed in the post-Easter situation or, strictly speaking, within the primitive church of the earliest period" (63).

133. J. Munck, "Paul, the Apostles, and the Twelve," 108.

134. Contra H. Tödt, The Son of Man in the Synoptic Tradition, 63. Tödt concludes on the basis of Judas' inclusion in the group of the twelve "that Jesus during his earthly activity had already summoned a group of 'the twelve' in particular" (ibid.). Judas' betrayal of Jesus may indeed be regarded as a pre-Easter event of historical provenance (Ph. Vielhauer, "Gottesreich und Menschensohn in der Verkündigung Jesu," Aufsätze zum Neuen Testament [München: Kaiser Verlag, 1965], 70; cf. B. Gärtner, Iscariot, tr. by Victor I. Gruhn [Philadelphia: Fortress Press, 1971], 13). But it is important to note that it was a psalm (Ps. 41:9) which enabled the later church to overcome apologetically the embarrassment which Judas' betrayal of Jesus must have meant for the community's christology. Jesus' allegedly intimate relationship with Judas (a relationship first prompted by Ps. 41:9) was later worked back into Jesus' earthly life. "Once the post-Easter group of the twelve had been dated back into Jesus' life, it was taken for granted that also the disciple who had betrayed him was a part of this group" (Ph. Vielhauer, "Gottesreich und Menschensohn in der Verkündigung Jesu," 71). Hence, "the association of Judas with the twelve is a theological postulate; but this postulate is nonetheless no historical proof for the pre-Easter existence of the twelve" (ibid. 71). It must be remembered that theological portrayals owe at least as much to reflection as to history itself. Historically, free-lance 'wandering charismatics' undoubtedly preached the coming kingdom during the early post-Easter period of the Christian community. The tradition, however, transferred to them the religious characteristics endemic to the traditional Son of Man sayings (G. Theissen, The First Followers of Jesus, 27).

P A R T   T W O

THE MYSTERIOUS TWELVE IN
THREE EARLY TRADITIONS

The appearance of twelve followers of Jesus in three
independent strands of the early Christian tradition adds
substance and depth to our understanding of the formative
stages of Christianity. The first of these is the pre-
Pauline tradition. It accords a post-Easter appearance of
the Lord to an anonymous group of twelve (1 Cor 15:5). Paul
cites this tradition in his Corinthian correspondence to
prove the historicity of Jesus' resurrection as it is attested in one of the New Testament's earliest christological
formulas (1 Cor 15:3f).[1] The two or three basic parts of
this early post-Easter formula undoubtedly contribute to our
knowledge of the christological and church-political develop-
ments in the pre-Pauline communities.[2] However, the confessional formula itself does not shed any light on the possible
historical role of these twelve individuals either during
Jesus' pre-Easter ministry or in the early post-Easter periods of the Christian church. Neither Paul himself nor any
other pre-Pauline figure ever refers to 'the twelve' in any
informed fashion. Paul met Cephas in Jerusalem at the time
of his first visit (Gal. 1:18f) but even then 'the twelve'
must have retired already from active church service.[3]

In the pre-Markan tradition, 'the twelve' are, in contrast to their pre-Pauline counterparts, a pre-Easter group,
remembered only as twelve bare names, Judas always being directly or indirectly included.[4] The lack of information on
the actual work of these twelve pre-Easter figures prompted
the evangelist Mark to give them a concrete place within the
context of his gospel.[5] Due to Mark's redactional efforts,
they are abidingly in Jesus' company, always ready to be instructed in the secrets of the kingdom which, in turn, they
continually fail to understand, but nonetheless they are
sent out to engage in some form of pre-Easter missionary work

(Mk. 3:13-19).[6] Significantly, the pre-Markan list itself
does not at all assign to them any missionary role. Moreover,
it is conspicuous that neither the pre-Markan nor the Markan
tradition has retained any single detail about their alleged
pre-Easter or post-Easter missionary activity in Palestine or
any other place outside of it. They must have disappeared
from the pages of history even before the earliest Christian
mission ever got under way. Who were they historically if
they managed to melt away so mysteriously? Or did their 'institution' collapse before they could etch their names in any
concrete fashion on any of the early Christian traditions?[7]
What became of these twelve figures is indeed, as the otherwise so cautious B. H. Streeter put it, "one of the mysteries
of history."[8] There is no easy solution to this mystery.
G. Theissen's assumption that the sudden disappearance of the
twelve was probably due to the group's early dispersion "to
all points of the compass"[9] is not a real solution but a
petitio principii, coming close to being a 'cover story'
which further mystifies the mystery of their strange disappearance from the stages of history. And Charles H. Talbert's
pastoral advice not to depreciate these twelve "as narrow,
nationalistic and lacking in vision"[10] is at best a piece of
well-meant guess work which first derives its strength and
substance from the embarrassing fact that absolutely nothing
in detail is known about them.

The Q Source is the third early Christian tradition which
refers to 'the twelve'. Q speaks neither of their pre-Easter
missionary role nor of their post-Easter experiences with the
risen Lord. In Q, it is the pre-Easter Jesus himself who
promises them a most dazzling career in the closing stages of
temporal history. In the end of days, the Q twelve will occupy twelve seats in the councils of the Son of Man. They are
promised then to assist the celestial Lord in his eschatological activity of meting out punishment to the twelve tribes
of Israel.[11] Similar claims are familiar from the literature
of the Qumran community, whose leaders also believed, as

G. Vermes states, that in the critical days of the imminent
Last Judgment their community would participate "in the
great battles of Light against Darkness."[12] But whereas the
Qumran claims had their setting within a concrete and historically identifiable community, the claims of the Q twelve
hang entirely in limbo. Neither a community rule nor any
community prayer or hymn bespeaks their actual role within
early Christianity. It is not even clear whether the Q
Source speaks of twelve individuals or merely of the twelve-
consciousness of the community itself.[13]

     A group that does not appear anywhere historically can-
not be subjected to a historical examination. The claim that
Jesus had appointed them during his earthly ministry is, in
view of the absence of historical evidence, anything but
self-evident.[14] The Christian twelve stand from the first
'above' history, exercising their authority not from within
the historical context of the church but rather from within
the compass of tradition theology, and the two should not be
confused. In this section of our study, it is our purpose
to examine the theological significance of this group against
the backdrop of the cultural climate within which the Christian communities have established their roots. It is our
hope to cast light on the origin of the Christian twelve idea
by focusing attention on the significance of the figure of
twelve in both Hellenistic and Jewish culture.

CHAPTER I
THE IRRESISTIBLE POWER OF
AN AMBITIOUS NUMBER

Numbers are vehicles for determining the numerical value
of tangible or intangible objects, as well as for measuring
and reckoning time. Number sequences establish and assert
the rich relationships between pure numerical magnitudes.
These specific relationships, however, do not exhaust at all
the significance which numbers have had in life. The history
of culture and religion brings to light that besides their
purely mathematical function numbers have at all times inspired the human mind to interweave them symbolically with
the most basic experiences in life. The small step from
mathematical number sequences to philosophical number systems
is well delineated by Hippolyt in his refutation of the various gnostic teachings of his day. Noting what R. McL. Wilson
rightly called "the gnostic penchant for numerical symbolism,"[15]
Hippolyt accuses the gnostics of capitalizing on Pythagoras.
They argue, he says, that the monad "is the father of the duad,
and the duad the mother of all things that are being begot-
ten."[16] Archetypal male and female roles are here represented
by numbers. As Hippolyt again observes, "if any, beginning to
number, says one, and adds two, then in like manner three,
these together will be six, and to these add moreover four,
the entire sum, in like manner, will be ten. For one, two,
three, four, become ten, i.e., the perfect number."[17] Even
though Hippolyt took issue here with the position of the gnostics, his statements portray with great clarity the way in
which the ancients made use of numbers. The choice of numer-
als undoubtedly differs greatly from one ancient writer to the
other. Philo shows a great liking, for instance, for the six,
the seven and the ten.[18] The Valentinians dwelled on the
thirty years of the Lord's hidden life on earth which, according to them, prefigured the total number of aeons.

> These divide into two groups of twelve and eighteen.
> The former are found in the number of disciples, the
> age at which our Lord paid His visit to the Temple.
> . . . The remaining group are represented in the
> eighteen months after the Resurrection during which,
> according to one tradition, our Lord taught Gnosis
> to his disciples.[19]

By contrast, the second-century gnostic Marcus based his system, as J. M. Hull has demonstrated, more "on the magical
powers of the alphabet and the mystic relationships between
their numbers, names and sounds."[20] Non-Christian philoso-
phers of the third century saw things again differently:

> There are twenty-four hours in the day and twenty-
> four letters in the Greek alphabet. Every letter
> equals an hour and is therefore an image of divin-
> ity. The alpha-omega, like the sum of the hours,
> represents the power of God in his totality.[21]

Number sequences were not only applied to all sorts of
daily affairs. From the beginning of cultural history, they
have invited the religious and the philosophical mind to
transform numerical magnitudes into number principles and
number systems, assisting man in his attempt to understand
better his place within both the visible and invisible world.
As Christoph J. Scriba has stated, numbers have always been
tools supporting man in his search for some deeper truth.[22]
Isidore of Serville (600 C.E.) put it neatly, Tolle numerum
omnibus rebus et omnia pereunt (take from all things their
number, and they all shall perish).[23] In the biblical world,
some of the numbers pregnant with deeper meaning are the
three, the four, the seven and the twelve. Admittedly, at
first all these numbers functioned only as purely mathematical entities. The Near Eastern mentality, however, promoted
them very early to higher echelons, converting them into mystical round numbers apt to throw a veil of semi-divinity over
all otherwise purely cultural phenomena.

a) The Number Twelve in Hellenistic Milieux

No lengthy documentation is necessary for the fact that
the figure of twelve has indelibly imprinted itself on the

cultural and religious mind of antiquity. The adoption of
the Babylonian talent as the equivalent of sixty minae (μναῖ)
had secured the number 'twelve' a firm place within the mone-
tary system of ancient Greece.[24] Since 'sixty' can be divided
by 'five' without remainder, the 'twelve', apart from its many
other functions, became one of the pillars within the Greek
numerical system. The place of the 'twelve' in Babylonian
astrology, about which we will have to say more later, rein-
forced the importance of the number even in the Greek market-
places. Examples illustrating the mystical significance of
the number in the religio-cultural life of Greece and Rome
are legion. K. Menninger's limited list of early Mediterranean twelve concepts is sufficient evidence for the distinguished place occupied by this symbolic number.

> Twelve vultures appeared as an omen to Romulus, the
> founder of the city of Rome, indicating that it was
> to last for 1200 years. The number 12 is also sig-
> nificant in Greek history: Homer relates that Ajax
> and Odysseus each commanded 12 ships; the 12 Ionian
> cities formed an alliance; 120 Boeotian sailors
> made up a ship's crew. And when we learn, further,
> that Menelaus was lord over 60 ships and recall the
> swineherd Eumeaus' 360 pigs . . ., we realize that
> the round number 12 belongs to the same category as
> the round number 60 and its multiples.[25]

K. Menninger's examples may have prompted R. de Vaux to provide additional illustrations which further demonstrate the
prestige of the number in Greek culture.

> En Grèce les groupes de douze personnes, animaux ou
> choses, reviennent fréquemment dans la littérature,
> la légende et le culte, Éole et Nélée ont douze en-
> fants, on dédie douze vaches à Athéna, douze taureaux
> à Poséidon, il y a douze travaux d'Hercule, douze
> Titans, douze grand dieux de l'Olympe. . . . A Rome,
> il y a aussi douze grands dieux du Panthéon, douze
> Frères Arvales, douze Luperques, le loi des Douze
> Tables, etc.[26]

Independently of K. Menninger and R. de Vaux, M. P.
Nilsson has called attention to the significance of the
'twelve' in the history of the Greek religion. On the
twelfth Artemision, the name of a spring month dedicated to

the goddess Artemis, the people of Magnesia sacrificed a bull
to Zeus Sosipolis, praying at the same time for a good harvest
and for the peace in that region. In the procession, preceding the sacrifice itself, homage was paid to the 'twelve gods',
whose images were carried on the shoulders of the worship-
pers.[27] Furthermore, Plato cites the decrees of the delphic
oracle which entail each city state to bring monthly sacri-
fices to one of the same gods consecutively.[28] The twelve
indeed has had an exciting history of its own, long before
Christianity ever appeared on the religious horizon of antiquity. It certainly was not Jewish or Christian writers
who first escorted the figure of twelve triumphantly into the
arenas of Mediterranean culture or religion. The number has
made the spotlight in both the Orient and the Latin world,
long before any of the twelve Christian apostles had made
their début!

The rapid advance of the Christian religion into the
Mediterranean world suggests that at a very early stage of
its history, the Christian movement must have come in touch
with the breadth and depth of Greek-Roman twelve symbolism,
for which, as we have seen, ample evidence can be produced.
It is mistaken to presume that the New Testament twelve concept must under all circumstances derive from the Jewish
tradition. As Jacques-É. Ménard has argued, Christian concepts

> ne sont pas nécessairement significatives d'une in-
> fluence juive bien déterminée ni bien particularisée.
> . . . A côté de réminiscences biblique, on y trouve
> des emprunts à tout ce qui circulait d'écrits et de
> traditions dégradé dans les milieux de petite et de
> moyenne culture.[29]

Why should it not be possible that the Latin penchant
for the figure of twelve may have inspired early Christianity
to create a Christian twelve concept? But a few consider-
ations must give us pause here. To conclude from the unde-
niable occurrence of the twelve in Mediterranean cultures
that the antecedents of the New Testament twelve should be

sought in Greece and Rome alone would be an intolerably rash
judgment.   This view would overlook the possibility that
even before setting foot on Hellenistic soil the wandering
Christian missionaries[30] might have had a twelve concept of
Jewish provenance.   Moreover, should it really be enough to
say that some general Christian liking for number plays motivated the assimilation of the various Mediterranean twelve
concepts into the Christian heritage?   Important as the usage
of the symbolic number undoubtedly was in the ancient Graeco-
Roman world, its prestige in the ancient world does not in
itself account for the role the New Testament twelve have
played in the Christian tradition.   The appearance of the
figure of the twelve in Latin cultures does not prove yet
that post-Easter Christianity actually borrowed its twelve
concept from there.   Possible contacts with the Greek-Roman
concepts can hardly be ruled out antecedently, any more than
Christian contacts with the first century Rabbinic tradition
can be ruled out on principle.   But the possibility of such
contacts is no evidence yet for truly existing conceptual
interrelationships.

It is necessary to say a word here about the way in
which any interpenetration of, or interaction between, analo-
gous religious or cultural phenomena can be tested.   The syncretistic fabric of the Christian religion[31] strongly attests
to the great openness of Christianity to any religious facet
that could genuinely enrich or edify the spiritual life of
the community.   It is one of the distinctive features of
Christianity that it has been able to assimilate so much that
originally had been quite alien to it.   To adapt itself to
the moral values of the surrounding cultures has been a char-
acteristic of the Christian religion.   So has the attempt to
borrow from non-Christian sources anything that is, as the
apostle Paul put it, "true, honourable, just, pure, lovely
or gracious" (Phil. 4:8).   This incontestable openness of
Christianity to syncretistic expansion has prompted E. Hatch
to state categorically that

> many usages which have prevailed and continue to pre-
> vail in the Christian Church are in reality Greek
> usages changed in form and colour by the influences
> of primitive Christianity, but in their essence
> Greek still.[32]

In the light of this, the possibility that Christianity may
have borrowed its twelve symbolism from Greek or Roman sources
can hardly be rejected on principle. The shortcomings of
such assumption, however, nonetheless still stand out most
sharply.

The hypothesis that the Christian community may have
borrowed its twelve concept from Greece or Rome is plausible
only in the abstract. It is unable to explain, however, how
and why the shapers of the Christian tradition would have
preferred the well-familiar Greek-Roman 'twelve' to all the
other equally familiar Latin mystical round numbers, such as
the three or the seven. Religious ideas, as well as symbolic
numbers, are never picked up merely for the fun of it. Any
adoption of a non-Christian concept was, as E. Hatch rightly
observed, "assimilation by, and absorption into existing
[italics mine] elements."[33] "New ideas and new motives"
mingle "with the waters of existing currents."[34] It was not
that the Mediterranean twelve concept gave rise to the Christian predilection for the symbolic use of the twelve. Instead, a church equipped already with its own twelve concept
was by necessity inclined to adopt any of the non-biblical
twelve configurations which widely circulated in the contemporary Mediterranean world. The very occurrence of a religious phenomenon in the non-Christian world does in itself
not prove yet that a seemingly similar Christian concept is
of non-Christian origin. It is rather necessary first to
identify the stimuli within the New Testament tradition which
in turn may have prompted the Christian mind to make use of
these phenomena. Which, then, were the 'existing' elements
in Christianity that lent themselves most readily to the
adoption of the non-Christian twelve tradition? Before responding to this question, another word of caution is in order.

The fact that the hypothesis of the Greek-Roman origin of the New Testament twelve concept cannot readily be authenticated is in itself no support at all for the traditional assumption that the appointment of twelve earthly disciples must go back to Jesus himself. Such a conclusion would be as rash as the attempt to derive the concept from Greek or Roman sources. To keep things in perspective, we have to point out here that the early Hellenistic Christian syncretists never tired of tampering with both the cosmological and soteriological ramifications of the symbolic number twelve. The Lord's appointment of twelve apostles corresponds, say the Clementine Homilies, to the sequence of twelve solar months, just as John the Baptist's alleged thirty disciple-leaders reflect the monthly reckoning of the moon.[35] These half-astrological, half-religious references, which could easily be multiplied, are the result of intermingling biblical with non-biblical twelve speculations. In its usage of the twelve, the growing church could indeed count on the universally appreciated prestige of that number. The figure of the twelve was liked by Christians and non-Christians alike for its wide range of religious and philosophical meanings. Whatever the rationale for the Christian adoption and formation of the twelve concept may have been, once the number had been introduced into the Christian tradition, it no longer needed the support of any biblical tradition, historical or not. It rather could stand on its own feet, associating itself with the 'twelve mentality' of the Mediterranean world. Once the Christian twelve concept had appeared in Christian faith, for whatever reason, it could thrive in its own way, due to the universal vim of this number in the thought-systems of the surrounding cultures.

The materials that have been surveyed in this chapter are intended to bring to light the fact that long before prospering within the structures of the Christian faith, and without any mediation of Judaism, the figure of twelve had established a solid reputation of its own in the Hellenistic milieu.

But now, if the appearance of the twelve in Greek-Roman culture, although accounting in part for the popularity of this
number in later Christian circles, does still not sufficiently
explain the reasons for its adoption into the Christian tradition, what then made the early Christian writers so keen
about the figure of twelve? To this question we shall now
turn our attention.

b) Number Symbolism in Jewish Culture

Christian faith originated from the claim that the same
Jesus who ended his life on a cross had reappeared to his
disciples, and that he continued to address himself as the
risen Christ-Lord to his people through the very word of the
cross. As a religion born in Palestine the early post-Easter
community could not but participate in the mental attitudes
controlling the life of the Middle East. The calendar of
this world had been determined for centuries by the astrological system of the zodiac. O. E. Neugebauer describes
the zodiac as "equal areas of the apparent orbital circle of
the sun," i.e., as the so-called ecliptic which, for the
ancients, delineated the imagined course travelled by the sun
on the celestial sphere.[36] The zodiac, symbolized by twelve
zodiacal signs, was for the Babylonians the narrow zone of
those parts of the heavens "within which lie the paths of the
sun, moon and principal planets."[37] The Greeks later made
the Babylonian zodiac the basis of their own calendar, chang-
ing only the position of the vernal equinox from the first
(Capricornus) to the middle (Aries) of the zodiacal signs.[38]
All Near Eastern and Western religious systems of twelve relate in one form or the other to the controlling power of the
Babylonian calendar which, in turn, was based on astrological
observations.[39]

It must be noted here that the ancient calendar was much
more than a vehicle for describing sidereal movements or for
measuring time. For ancient men the world itself rested upon
the constellations of the firmament. They therefore singled

out the luminary bodies, the stars and particularly the
twelve signs of the zodiac, assigning to them a most dominant
place in worship. In antiquity, says F. Cumont to the point,
"the centuries, the years and the seasons, placed into relation with the four winds . . ., the twelve months connected
with the zodiac, the day and the night, the twelve hours, all
were personified and deified."[40] Born in Babylon and reared
in the temples of Syria and Egypt, ancient astrology infil-
trated and permeated all spheres of Near Eastern life, religious and secular, exercising an almost uncontested domination
over them all. It is not that astrology as "the first scien-
tific theology"[41] preceded only the appearance of Christianity.
The number twelve had established its spiritual empire long
before the ancient Israelites even began to move into the
cultural land of Palestine. M. Noth and N. Gottwald have re-
affirmed what has long been acknowledged by historians of
religion: that the astrological principles of ancient Babylon
still linger on in some form within the deeper structures of
Israel's sacred twelve tribe system.[42] Astrological principles had forced themselves upon the Canaanite religion, upon
Persian Mazdaism, as well as upon Egyptian sun worship. Small
wonder, even Israel could not elude their powerful grip. The
appearance of the number twelve within Israel's tribal structure is an unmistakable sign of it.

It goes without saying that in terms of immediate moti-
vations, the interrelationship between the Babylonian zodiac
and the ancient Israelite clan system was at no point a direct
one. Not the fascination with astral phenomena but rather
concrete historical experiences must have given rise to the
confederate system of ancient Israel, whatever that system
may have been in detail. The recourse to the zodiac only explains the unchallenged prestige of the figure twelve within
the context of Near Eastern cultures, and its interpretive
usefulness within the biblical religion. The immediate reasons for the creation of Israel's tribal alliance must re-
side, as M. Noth has shown, in the historical experiences of

the inner-Palestine (Leah-) clans, originally perhaps only
loosely connected on the one hand, and those of the more ag-
gressive Joseph tribe, probably coming from outside Palestine,
on the other. Scholars critical of M. Noth's reconstruction
of Israel's premonarchic, preconfederate and perhaps even pre-
settlement tribal history no longer maintain that early Israel
ever was a twelve-tribe association. They rather prefer to
describe the alliance more in socioeconomic than in religious
terms. For N. Gottwald, for instance, the early alliance was
not of amphictyonic nature but rather "a protective association" of social entities "built around the extended family
as the prime socioeconomic unit but extending to higher levels
of organization in the form of . . . tribal units."[43] But
even this description acknowledges, and this alone is of interest here, that a series of mutually shared early historical experiences brought racially interrelated groups into
some sort of a confederacy.

The image of a neatly organized twelve tribe alliance,
at all times acting in concert, stems from a much later time.
Only in retrospect was Israel considered, as A. Bettelheim
has noted, a perfect unity "consisting of twelve tribes, cor-
responding to the twelve sons of Jacob-Israel."[44] The deuteronomistic image of the clans, cooperating in warfare and
united in every respect when their most vital interests were
at stake,[45] is, as M. Noth has observed, a late idealization
of Israel's alleged golden age.[46] Yet given the artificial-
ity[47] of the way in which the deuteronomistic history de-
scribed the ancient tribal alliance,[48] the fact of David's
success, for instance, in consolidating the nation shows that
the early tribal confederacy cannot be assigned to the world
of fiction alone. In his efforts to unite the country, David
could fall back on a strong intertribal consciousness. Of a
fictitious nature are the later descriptions of the alliance,
but not the historical experiences themselves, leading up to
its formation. The sixth-century Deuteronomist, intent on
giving a theological explanation of the two national disasters

of 721 and 587 B.C.E., could not fall back on any personal
experience with the tribal system itself, any more than the
synoptics could flesh out their portrayals of Jesus' association with his disciples from first-hand experience. The
Deuteronomist had before him at best a handful of fragmentary
records from earlier periods, as well as some archival tribal
lists, perhaps from a book of genealogies.[49] He had to use
his own imagination to build these materials into his overall
conception of Israel's covenantal history as a downward pro-
gression from earlier obedience to Yahweh to later impudent
rejection of his sovereignty. Nonetheless, the deuteronomistic attempt to interpret all the earlier reminiscences of
Israel's ancient history within the framework of an imaginary
yet well-organized sacral clan alliance was still by no means
sheer fiction. Whatever the early tribal community may have
been, rich historical experiences undoubtedly stand behind
all the later monarchical images of the twelve tribe union.[50]
What the evidence submitted here brings to light is that the
figure of twelve, itself firmly rooted in Near Eastern astrology, functioned in Israel's historiography as an effective
vehicle enabling the biblical writers to understand their own
past in terms of a divinely ordained history. A few additional remarks are in order here about the interpretive power
of the 'twelve' within and without the immediate context of
Israel.

Early Israel was not the only ancient community that had
organized itself on the socio-religious model of a tribal confederacy. Similar alliances seem to have been part and parcel
of Israel's surrounding culture. According to old and mostly
priestly lists, frequently standing unconnected like erratic
boulders within the narrative context of the book of Genesis,
not only Jacob but also Nahor, the Aramaean, the brother of
Abraham, had twelve sons, eight from his wife Milcah and four
from his concubine Reumah.[51] Ishmael, Abraham's son from the
Egyptian maid Hagar,[52] had likewise organized his twelve
descendants in a twelve-village alliance. The list calls

these descendants the "twelve princes according to their
tribes."[53] By the same token, Keturah, Abraham's second wife,
had according to the Jahvist[54] six sons[55] who, in turn, perhaps even with Abraham's blessing, seem to have lived in a
tribal (six) settlement in the east country. A twelve tribe
system of some sort seems also to stand behind the Edomite
list[56] recorded in the priestly context of Gen. 36:10-14.
The J-list of the "sons of Seir the Horite,"[57] which like all
the other lists bears, for G. von Rad, the stamp of authenticity,[58] seems to describe another of the early tribal alliances. Precise twelveness cannot be claimed for the Horite
community. But this may be due to the fact that the list
contains doublets. Such doublets, says von Rad, appear in
most ancient documents.[59] It is important to note that in
all these lists, the respective clans have, in typically ancient fashion, traced back their history to the growth of one
single family. It all begins with a patriarch whose twelve
(or six) sons grow into clans, tribes and sometimes even king-
doms.[60] In this system of thought, the sacred origin of a
later socioeconomic, political or religious institution is
highlighted by the vision of twelve ancestral founder figures who, in turn, bespeak the zodiacal permanence of the
stellar movements. N. Gottwald is therefore right in suggesting that in antiquity the twelve was a number connoting totality and wholeness, as is "reflected in the division of the
heavens into twelve parts."[61]

        Whether or not all the non-Israelite lists really
reach back into the premonarchic or even preconfederate periods of Israel's history is of no great significance in the
context of this inquiry. While G. von Rad had still derived
these lists from an ancient yet hypothetical 'book of genealogies',[62] N. Gottwald tends to describe them as late 'pseudo-
genealogies',[63] a view that has recently been rejected by
C. Westermann.[64] But even N. Gottwald allows for some old
memories to be retained in these lists,[65] although for the
most part he assigns them to the hand of a literarily very

productive but as well highly hypothetical 'traditionalist',[66] said to have twelveness systematically inserted into the available ancient records of the non-Israelite tribal organizations. The reference to the twelve Ishmaelite princes[67] thus is nothing more, says Gottwald, than the P-writer's dramatic imposition of Israel's theological twelve image on the Ishmaelite units.[68] The minutiae of these assumptions are beyond the scope of this study. Our brief comments are merely intended to indicate that Old Testament scholarship has to provide much more information before the alleged existence of such 'traditionalist' can be authenticated. In its present form the precarious traditionalist-hypothesis seems to affirm rather than to discredit the old age of the Semitic lists.[69] Without denying, then, that in some instances twelveness may indeed be of reflective rather than historical origin, we still do not wish to rule out the possibility that some tribal (twelve?) confederacies, similar to that of early Israel itself, may have flourished in ancient Palestine. As a symbolically rich number, the twelve was as precious to these non-Israelite tribal groupings as to Israel itself. To what extent, if at all, these communities availed themselves of the interpretive power of the twelve can however, at this distance of time, no longer be ascertained.

Phenomenologically, the Semitic alliances of Palestine have their most striking counterparts in the politico-religious city-leagues of the ancient Graeco-Roman world. Although it cannot be said that all the Mediterranean leagues were twelve-member coalitions, the figure of the twelve nonetheless played a dominant role in the constitution of most of them.[70] The (Thermo)pylaean-Delphic twelve member amphictyony, for example, first took care of the Demeter shrine of Anthela, and later shifted its attention to the more important Apollon-temple on Delos, as M. P. Nilsson has shown.[71] M. Noth has listed, among others, the twelve-member coalition of Onchestos in Boeotia, the alliance of twelve Ionic cities worshipping at the central shrine on the island of Mycale, off the coast of eastern Asia

Minor, as well as the <u>duodecim populi</u> of the Etruscans mentioned also in Livius' writings.[72] Whatever the socio-religious differences between the more democratically organized
Greek amphictyonies and the law-oriented Semitic alliances
may have been, the appearance of twelveness in both types of
systems shows that the zodiacal prestige of the twelve has
left its marks on western as well as on eastern confederacies.
Even some indo-germanic tribes of northern Europe seem to
have found the twelve-clan alliance still attractive enough
to fashion their own communal life on it, as R. de Vaux has
pointed out persuasively.[73] All these formations were undoubtedly the result of long and complex historical experiences assuring these communities of the firmness of their
common beliefs. A common language and the challenges of common enemies must also have contributed greatly to the stability of these alliances whose founders, and later custodians,
in reflecting back on their own history, at one point must
have begun to conceive of the leagues in terms of twelveness.
Historically, none of them ever began with exactly twelve-
member cities or clans. Conscious of the mysterious relation
which existed for all ancients, Orientals or Latins, between
earthly religio-political events and the sidereal deities,[74]--
the latter being considered as inexhaustible generators of
energy--the figure of the twelve was, perhaps with the seven,[75]
a most welcome symbolic tool by which to invest a political
coalition with the aura of divine permanence. Joint actions
in history, initially born out of political necessity, had
given rise to a new self-consciousness on the part of the par-
ticipants acting in concert. Twelveness later both interpreted
and institutionalized the bonds which continued to unite the
members of these alliances. Twelveness gave them their own
secret from the heavens.

The view, advocated by M. Noth and G. von Rad, that
there existed some direct historical link between the Israelite twelve-tribe confederacy and the sacral cultic leagues of
ancient Greece[76] is no longer shared by the mainstream

contemporary Old Testament scholars. "The amphictyony is not a proper model to apply to Israel's overall confederate design," says N. Gottwald in the conclusion of his extensive study of the peculiar traits of both systems.[77] The weight given to the location of the central shrine, as well as the cultic regulations binding on all league-members, is so different in both types of twelve-alliances that any form of historical interaction between them must be ruled out from the first.[78] Since the Greek-Roman amphictyonic coalitions were at no point of history legal communities but merely federations concerned with the protection of a common cult and the mitigation of warfare among the member city-states, the designation 'amphictyony', if applied to the Israelite tribal system, would not adequately describe what was constitutive for Israel's tribal system proper. "To designate the Israelite clan system," says R. de Vaux in agreement with N. Gottwald, "as an 'amphictyony' cannot but confuse the issue and must engender misconceptions with regard to inter-tribal relationships."[79]

It must be noted here that R. de Vaux' objections are directed only to M. Noth's attempt to connect the Israelite twelve-tribe system with the Greek amphictyonic structure. His concern is not to dismantle the overarching ancient twelve-tribe confederacy but rather to establish its Semitic uniqueness. "L'emploi du mot 'amphictyonie' à propos Israël," he states, "ne peut qu'engendrer la confusion."[80] The prominence of Israel's tribal scheme, relating already at its formative stages to some type of twelveness, is uncontested in R. de Vaux' studies. The recent renewed inquiry into the historical date of Israel's twelve-tribe confederacy is the immediate result of the collapse of M. Noth's amphictyonic hypothesis. If the twelve-tribe scheme was not fashioned on Greek models, when and why, then, did Israel single out the figure of twelve for highlighting the sacredness of its confederacy? It is difficult to say at this distance of time whether the adoption of the twelvefold tribal pattern really

reaches back into the time of the early covenantal celebration
at Shechem (Jos. 24). The absence of any uncontested pre-
Davidic references to the twelve-tribe system has prompted
N. Gottwald to doubt this.[81] He therefore reduced M. Noth's
imagined premonarchic twelve-clan confederacy, with its root-
age in the Greek-Latin amphictyonic structure, to a relatively pale union of initially only very loosely organized Semitic
tribes.[82] Not even the Jahvist, Gottwald states, had any
first-hand knowledge of the coalition of exactly twelve-member
clans,[83] let alone the shapers of the tradition before him.
The appearance of monarchic institutions in David's (or possibly Saul's) time,[84] first contributed to the eventual re-
casting of the reminiscences about the early tribal confeder-
ation "into a fixed twelve-tribe scheme."[85] Israel's twelve-
tribe system thus is, in N. Gottwald's perspective, nothing
other than the late conceptual correlate of a much earlier
loose social organization of an odd number of tribes.[86] What
we are saying here is that whereas for earlier Old Testament
research the symbolic number had interpreted the premonarchic
historical association of the tribes, N. Gottwald contests
the pre-Davidic origin of the twelve-clan system. He rather
relates the origin of Israel's twelveness to the interpretive
efforts of the monarchy's self-conscious court historians.

The exact date of Israel's adoption of the twelvefold
tribal pattern can be left open in our study. In this chapter we have shown that the zodiacal number had been firmly
established in the Oriental world long before the Israelite
tribes ever began to consolidate themselves in the cultural
land. Even if the twelve-tribe system should predate the
time of the united monarchy, which is still possible, the
well-established sacred number offered its services to the
premonarchic founding fathers as well as it would otherwise
have commended itself to the court historians. The important
thing is that once the number had made its début on the stages
of Israel's history, premonarchic or monarchic, its indispu-
table grandeur began automatically to impose on all sectors of

Israel's culture and religion. It is hardly accidental that
in the deuteronomistic writings twelve followers of Saul's
son Ishboshet contended with twelve servants of David, on the
verge of the united monarchy (2 Sam 2:15). The victory of
the latter heralded the birth of a strong united kingdom.
The prestige of the figure of twelve also influenced the country's administrative patterns. It is an unmistakable allusion
to Israel's tribal system when King Solomon put the new department for Royal Food Supplies into the hands of twelve
high-ranking officers, each responsible for providing the
king's household with food on a monthly rota (1 K 4:7).
Whether these references stem from the sixth-century Deuteronomist himself or go back to earlier memories, they all
bring to light the lasting popularity of the celestial twelve
throughout the centuries. The statues of twelve lions standing on each side of six steps leading up to Solomon's ivory
throne (1 K 10:20) represent an interesting architectural
variation of the same twelve concept. The twelve lions pro-
tecting the throne here symbolically present the monarchy as
the legitimate heir of the former confederate tribal organization. All these examples, which could be multiplied,[87]
show how majestically the heavenly twelve predominated over
all sectors of Israel's monarchical life. The zodiacal
twelve had indeed become the queen of Israel's number system.
At no point, however, did the twelve derive its power from
factual twelvefoldness in Israel's institutional life, politi-
co-administrative or religious. Its credentials do not derive from historical factuality. The number rather invested
all ancient historical institutions with a transcendental
quality, needed in antiquity to make them immune to the ero-
sive power of temporality. The astrological figure of the
twelve, born long ago in the 'observatories' of ancient Babylon, highlighted and authenticated, within Israel and without,
religious claims made in history but not at all on the basis
of history.

Before turning our attention to the significance of
twelveness in the Qumran community, it is important to note
that the post-Easter Christian community, due to its Palestinian origin, participated fully in Israel's number symbolism. In New Testament times, the figure of twelve pulsated
in the veins of contemporary culture and religion. The preoccupation of the Christian community with this figure is anything but surprising in the light of the number's own long
history in Israel. The fact that the twelve-scheme was also
operative in Graeco-Roman symbolism,[88] as we have demonstrated
in the previous chapter, only enhanced its dignity, and made
it into an effective vehicle for the communication of the new
Christian claims. It now appeared (but only 'appeared'!) to
the Christian missionaries that the biblical number had mysteriously affected the 'pagan' cultures before the non-biblical world had even come in touch with the biblical faith. As
a symbolic number denoting totality, wholeness and unity, the
twelve continued to inspire the Christian witnesses, in the
same measure as it had kindled the imagination of their Israelite counterparts centuries before. We have seen earlier
that the twelve-tribe idea may in itself have been the conceptual correlate of an earlier, numerically undetermined
union of tribes. By the same token, the New Testament's
twelve-disciple pattern can also be regarded as the theological conceptualization of memories which, in some form, relate
back to the time of Jesus' earthly ministry. In the following chapters we will follow the lead of this suggestion. That
Jesus had attracted an odd number of followers with his eschatological kingdom proclamation does not at all create a
historical problem, irrespective of the fact that his occa-
sional association with sinners and tax-collectors has undoubtedly been stereotyped by the later Christian tradition.
What constitutes a serious historical problem is the claim
that the pre-Easter herald of God's 'imminent' kingdom had
himself appointed a neatly chosen group of just twelve
earthly disciple-apostles. Not even the earliest Christian

traditions support this assumption, as we have shown elsewhere.[89] In the light of the Oriental history with the zodiacal symbol sign, and its rich application to Israel's life,
any number other than the twelve would have inspired a higher
measure of historical confidence!

c) The Twelve in Qumran Writings

The zodiacal figure of twelve celebrated another of its
great religious feats in the history of the much-debated intertestamental Qumran community.[90] The Dead Sea Scrolls,
discovered between 1945 and 1956, in eleven caves on the
northwestern shore of the Dead Sea, have greatly contributed
to the reconstruction of the sect's ascetic community life,
and these documents must be consulted if we wish to understand the rationale for the brotherhood's use of our number.
It is most revealing that this law-oriented Jewish sectarian
group, which throughout displays a marked bias towards discipline and severity,[91] chose the symbolic number of twelve to
launch its own claims to ultimacy. As Th. H. Gaster has
pointed out, the Qumran covenanters viewed themselves as the
avant-garde of the 'true and ideal congregation of future
Israel'.[92] It must be understood that this claim, although
defiantly repudiated by contemporary orthodox Judaism,[93] was
nonetheless part of the scenario of all contemporary religious
groups, Jewish and non-Jewish. At the turn of the eras, Palestine saw an astonishing proliferation of eschatological
movements, each passionately claiming to have the only key to
the secrets of the end. The Hellenistic counterparts of
these movements were the mystery religions which, equally fer-
vently, initiated their adherents into the only true way to
salvation.[94] The Qumran sectaries constituted only one of
the many elitist movements which had mushroomed in the area,
zealously trying to keep their followers away from the evil
influences of the surrounding culture.[95] To say that the
sectaries had deemed themselves to be identical with the
righteous part of all humanity, as D. Flusser put it,[96] is

perhaps saying too much. The close-knit desert sectaries
did not give their particularistic hopes any touch of universalism. They claimed to be the eschatological and true
Israel, i.e., the community of Yahweh's elect,[97] without anticipating the universalistic outlook of the Christian or
any other Hellenistic movement. Significantly, although
Qumran's eschatological claims were undoubtedly 'visionary'
in nature, they did not at all spring from visions or audi-
tions, but rather from a life of unconditional obedience to
the stipulations of the Mosaic Law. The covenanters, most
probably identical with the Essenes mentioned in contemporary writings,[98] never wished to be anything but a _Jewish_
brotherhood community.

All the differences between the Qumran community and
orthodox Judaism notwithstanding,[99] the sectarian attempt to
make the Law into the absolute referent of the community's
life is well in keeping with the basic concerns and aspira-
tions of the entire Jewish religion. Already the Deuteronomist, convinced that both Israel's and Judah's blatant in-
difference to the Law had led to the tragedies of 721 and
587 B.C.E., hammered home to his befuddled contemporaries
that only resolute acts of renewed obedience could heal the
broken covenant relationship between Yahweh and his people.
In the same vein, the Chronicler and the Royal Psalms focused their attention upon the monarch sitting on his throne
to administer justice among the people (2 Chr 19). In the
Chronicler's view, the king's judicial exercise, carried out
in the presence of all the Jerusalem court prophets, was the
earthly replica of Yahweh's own celestial activity.[100] God
takes his place in the divine council, says Psalm 82, and he
holds judgment in the midst of his divine counsellors. The
prophets call upon the kings to fashion their exercise of
justice on this divine model. It is not only the concern
for fairness and impartiality in worldly matters which is
expressed in these references. In upholding justice in Israel (or Judah), the king and his appointed judges act rather

on behalf of Yahweh himself. "Consider what you do, for you
judge not for man but for the Lord," the Chronicler tells
the kings of Judah.[101] The earthly tribunals with the king
as the presiding officer are to correspond to the heavenly
courts with Yahweh presiding over 'the gods' (Ps. 82:1).

The king's judgmental functions, as depicted in these
post-exilic references, highlight the intentions of the ancient Urim and Thummim practices, recorded in the book of
Exodus.[102] The ancient laws, retained in this book, decree
that the priestly garments of Aaron and his sons must be
decorated with 'two onyx stones', with the twelve names of
the sons of Israel to be engraved upon them.[103] By the same
token, Aaron's 'breastplate of judgment', the receptacle of
the Urim and Thummim, is said to have been bedecked with four
rows of three precious stones each, the twelve stones together symbolizing not only Israel's totality as a tribal
union but also the impartial judgment guaranteed by divine
will to all 'the sons of Israel'.[104]

The firm commitment of the Qumran brotherhood to the Law
must be seen in the light of Israel's overall preoccupation
with covenantal concerns. The ultra-conservative sect was undoubtedly a religious phenomenon of its own, different in many
respects from other Jewish movements of the day. It nonetheless operated from the outset within the Jewish value-system,
as the reappearance of the 'breastplate', for instance, in the
War Rule strongly indicates.[105] Quite in contrast to the
Christian emphasis on a new or even better Law,[106] the Qumran
sectaries were unconditionally devoted to a thorough examination and reinterpretation of the Jewish Torah. The reappearance of the figure of twelve in Qumran literature is, in view
of the sect's commitment to the Law and its stipulations, anything but surprising. Even the ancient institution of the Urim
and Thummim received the renewed attention of this intertestamental group. It reappears in the slightly enigmatic _pesher_
on Isa. 54:11 (4QpIsa), which speaks of twelve chief priests
who 'give light by the judgment of the Urim and Thummim'.

['Behold, I will set your stones in antimony'. The
interpretation of this statement is that] [he will
ar]ray all Israel like antimony around the eye. 'And
lay your foundations with sapph[ires', this refers
to the ...], [wh]o founded the council of the community, the priests, and the lai[ty...], the congregation of his chosen one - like a sapphire among
stones. [As to that which is said, 'And I will make
as agate'], 'All your pinnacles', this refers to the
twelve [chief priests who] give light by the judge-
ment of the Urim and Thummim [...], which shine
forth (?) from them like the sun in all its radiance.
'And al[l your gates of carbuncle'], this refers to
the heads of the tribes of Israel in the [latter
days...], their allotted stations [...].[107]

The pesher casts an intense light on both the ideology
and the institutions of the Qumran community,[108] a brotherhood convinced of its participation in God's Last Judgment.[109]
D. Flusser has persuasively argued that John's visionary account of the heavenly Jerusalem (Rev. 21), with its twelve
gates, twelve foundations and twelve apostles, was fashioned
on the language of this pesher.[110]

It must be noted here that the law-oriented Qumran community consisted of two branch organizations, [111] both of which
were equally firm in their commitment to the programme of perfect obedience to the judgments of the Torah. The first
group is the seclusive, monastically structured male brotherhood of the Council of the Community, a group of sectaries
first and mainly engaged in the study and practice of the
Law.[112] The so-called Community Rule,[113] written perhaps in
the later half of the second century B.C.E.,[114] served as
some sort of catechism for these 'men of holiness', who were
extremely critical of orthodox Judaism. They enforced the
rule of common property-ownership on all the members,[115] and
considered the Second Temple as contaminated by wicked
priests.[116] These 'men of holiness' were under oath to keep
away from Jerusalem's 'worship of falsehood', [117] and to look
forward to the eschatological day when the purity of all divine offices would finally be restored.[118] The less rigidly
organized town sectaries[119] constitute the second branch group

of Qumran, which was subordinated to the seclusive desert
brotherhood. This town branch was much more practically inclined than the desert brothers, as the Damascus Rule indicates.[120] Neither the rules of celibacy nor those of common
ownership were imposed on the town fellowship.[121] They continued to live their life of obedience to the law within the
context of urban or rural Israel, subjected to the sect's
basic rules but still not entirely separated from Israel's
temple worship.[122]

We have seen earlier that pre-exilic Israel used the
zodiacal number to highlight the divine origin of its tribal
confederacy. The community of twelve tribes represents here
the totality and perfection of the heavenly world. Such a
community is unmistakably the apple of Yahweh's eye, reared
and protected by his divine hand. The two-branch Qumran
brotherhood, well conversant with the biblical imagery, reactivated the sacred number in order to present itself as the
true heir to the ancient desert community. It is patent from
both the Community Rule and the Damascus Rule that the sectaries regarded themselves with the highest measure of confidence as the true Israel of the future.[123] For these covenanters the eschatological war between the sons of light
(Qumran)[124] and the sons of darkness[125] was imminent. They
alleged that upon the victorious completion of this battle,
Israel would once again be restored to its former status of
a holy twelve-tribe community united, as in the beginnings
of Israel's history, under the rule of the divinely ordained
priesthood of the sons of Zadok. Since the Qumran 'visionaries' did not distinguish sharply between the community's
present reality and its future hopes,[126] its priestly leaders
did not hesitate to model the community's present religious
life on the eschatological order[127] of the future, a future
order which, in turn, was the replica of Israel's 'sacred
past'. The figure of the twelve thus appears in a variety of
contexts, legal, judicial or liturgical.[128] Its setting

proper in Qumran, however, is the context of promises which
all relate to the eschatological future of the community.

The community's eschatological hopes are spelled out in
the War Rule,[129] a writing that drew its inspiration from
Daniel's visions about eschatological battles to be fought
with the so-called Kittim of Assyria (Dan. 11:29f). The
prophet himself undoubtedly expected these battles to usher
in the new age. The covenanters gave the Danielic vision a
new measure of urgency by applying it to the Roman invasion.
The rising tensions between the Jewish and the Hellenistic
mentality prompted the brotherhood to combine Daniel's vision
with the idea of a forty-year-long eschatological war expected to be fought with the Romans.[130] In an ingenious act
of interpretation, the Qumran 'scribes' saw in the Assyrian
Kittim of Daniel's provenance the approaching armies of the
Romans. The Qumran warriors, recruited only from the physi-
cally fit,[131] dreamt that they would come out victoriously
from those battles in the seventh year of the great war.[132]
Since they were succoured and upheld by the mighty hand of
God, and by the power of the princely Angel of Michael,[133]
the victory could not but be on their side. It is in the
context of the eschatological battle-array that the figure
of the twelve appears. The Qumran warriors are said to go
into battle equipped with standards and shields bearing the
names of all twelve tribes. The scenario is reminiscent
of the holy war accounts of Joshua and the book of Judges.

> On the Great Standard at the head of the people
> they shall write, 'The People of God', together
> with the names of Israel and Aaron, and the names
> of the twelve [tribes of Israel]. . . . And on
> the sh[ields of] the Prince of the Congregation
> they shall write his name . . . and the names of
> the twelve tribes of Israel . . . with the names
> of their twelve chiefs.[134]

Once the sons of light had won the decisive battle in
their ongoing fight with the ungodly armies of 'the Prince
of the kingdom of wickedness',[135] the true Israel,[136] pre-

figured by Qumran's life in purity, would finally be identical with the Israel de facto, and the rift between physical and spiritual Israel would once and for all be healed. In the remaining thirty-three years of the forty-year battle, the warriors of renewed Israel would still continue their fight against the remnants of all sorts of partly imaginery and partly truly geographical nations,[137] yet without the final victory ever being in jeopardy again. The War Rule promises that after the completion of the eschatological battles, the seasons of righteousness will finally arrive, and the light of peace "shine over all the ends of the earth,"[138] going on shining until even the last shadows of darkness are removed. God's "exalted greatness," the War Rule prognosticates, "shall shine eternally to the peace . . . of all the sons of light."[139] It is in this connection that the twelve symbolism had again its effect on the community's outlook on the future. When God's righteousness is finally restored, then all Israel will be reorganized, and the institutions of the true Israel be re-established. In harmony with God's Torah, "twelve chief priests" will then occupy their seats below the Highpriest and his vicar, the twelve ministering "at the daily sacrifice before God."[140] Below them will be ranked the twelve chiefs of the Levites, one for each tribe, with the chiefs of the twelve tribes and the heads of the family.[141] The appointment of the twelve priests, mentioned earlier, is said to be made on the basis of their record of blowing the sacred 'trumpets of Massacre'[142] in the battles against the Kittim and their ungodly allies. After the final battle they will also provide leadership in Israel's everlasting liturgies of praise.[143] In these days of triumph, a new court of twelve, including the priests, will be established to guarantee justice among the tribes.[144] The king's council, mentioned in the Qumran ordinances, will then be reconvened after the long interval of inactivity during the rule of the wicked.[145] According to an excerpt from the Temple Scroll disclosed by Y. Yadin,

the Qumran visionaries even foresaw that in those days the
king would again have twelve chief advisors, and twelve
priests plus twelve Levites, appointed to counsel him in all
matters of the Torah.[146] It is patent from all these references that the covenanters were not concerned here with the
contemporary administration of the sect, but rather with offices to be filled and appointments to be made at a time
following the eschatological war. The covenanters envisioned
that the courts of future Jerusalem would then be structured
on the duodecimal principle so dominant in Israel's past.[147]
The hope in the restoration of the original twelvefold pattern was here undoubtedly determined by the ancient belief
that the end would be a replica of the beginning.[148] What
must be noted in this context is that Qumran's eschatological
hopes in the restoration of Israel's original perfect twelveness have also been allowed to spill over into the sect's contemporary structures of organization. Even in the present
yaḥad (gathering) the symbolic number occupied a place of
highest honour.

According to some strands of the Qumran materials, the
highest authority among the desert sectaries lay in the hands
of a Community Council which was presided over by the 'tri-
umvirate' of a Priest,[149] a Guardian, the so-called 'Head of
the Congregation' and the expert in instructional and judicial
matters,[150] and a Bursar, who was in charge of administrative
matters.[151] In other parts of the material, the Qumran Council itself was the highest court of authority in the community.
In this Council, so the Community Rule states,

> there shall be twelve men and three priests, perfectly
> versed in all that is revealed of the law . . . walk-
> ing with all men [of holiness] according to the stand-
> ard of truth and the rule of the time.[152]

The dignity and prestige of this Council appear in designations
such as 'Everlasting Plantation', 'House of Perfection and
Truth in Israel', 'House of Holiness for Israel', 'Assembly of
Supreme Holiness for Aaron', and witness to 'The Truth at the

Judgment'.[153] The Council, so we read, shall be "that tried
wall, that precious cornerstone whose foundations shall neither
rock nor sway in their place."[154] The absence of any systematic
exposition of the sect's constitution and its laws makes it
extremely difficult to determine the actual function of these
duodecim council members, especially in comparison with and
relation to the Priest, Guardian and Bursar. The Council itself is mentioned in all strands of the Qumran material, oc-
cupying pride of place throughout.[155] The 'twelve men and
three priests', however, appear only in chapter eight of the
Community Rule. Did they constitute the nucleus or minimum
quorum of the Council proper, a special elite group or a select deliberative body within the Council?[156]

Whatever their immediate role within the community's religious life may have been, the appearance of a body of twelve
men in the regulations of Qumran bespeaks the high measure of
interaction between the brotherhood's future hopes, as expressed in the War Rule and other eschatological writings, and
its ascetic community life in the Judean desert. The full
restoration of Israel's sacred twelveness was for Qumran definitely of a future date.[157] However, the twelve 'deputies' of
the desert Council seem to have anticipated this future in
their very person. They seem to have represented the imminence of the expected restoration of Israel's history. Inter-
estingly, the town sectaries placed very little weight on the
figure of the twelve. They rather substituted another number
for it. According to the Damascus Rule, the camp covenanters
had grouped themselves in actual or imaginary units of thou-
sands, hundreds, fifties or tens,[158] with a College of Ten
Judges[159] wielding ultimate authority among them.[160] This
judicial body, consisting of four priests and six laymen, was
responsible for upholding the Law among less rigidly organized lay units, and for carrying out the necessary discipli-
nary actions among them. Since the town covenanters were in
terms of cultic status not on a par with the dominant desert
community, the 'ten judges' undoubtedly had much less actual

authority than their (twelve/three) Council counterparts in
the desert. Similar to the twelve concept of the desert
brotherhood, the tenfold structure of the camp fellows was
equally rich in symbolic significance. The ten judges
symbolized the absolute authority of the Decalogue among
these 'town people of the camp'.[161] We encounter here again
the prominent function of Jewish number symbolism. Whether
the figure of the twelve or that of the ten, the number did
not primarily stand for an actually existing administrative
or governing body. In Israel as well as in Qumran, numbers
represented before anything else the deepest religious concerns and claims of the community.

No convincing evidence can be submitted for the contention that early Christianity has been in direct contact with
either of the two branches of Qumran. As D. Flusser observed,
no New Testament author proves himself to be directly and independently influenced by the Qumran sectarians (or by Jewish
circles close to them)."[162] But who could ignore the fact
that both groups shared the general Jewish mentality of the
time, and that both, each on the basis of its own presupposi-
tions, worked out its own positive or negative response to
the Jewish heritage?[163] The common denominator of Qumran and
the Jewish Christian Q community, says A. D. Jacobson in his
analysis of Q's Wisdom christology, was their common interest
in the reformation of Israel. "Like Qumran, the Q community
was a reformation movement within Israel."[164] Needless to
say, in developing their own religious ideas, the Qumran sect
and the various strands of the Christian movement each kept
to its own course. Each of the two was controlled by the inner logic of its own religious thinking. The Christian community paid closest attention to the conceptually rather complex kingdom proclamation of Jesus, interpreting it increas-
ingly in the light of the Christian post-Easter kerygma. The
powerful Qumran Council chose another route of approach and
took its cue from the early patterns of Israel's history,
viewing itself as the microcosmic anticipation of the future

macrocosmic twelve-tribe community of the renewed people of
God. Both movements wrote their own commentary on the nonetheless commonly shared complex Jewish heritage, though quite
independently of one another.

Although the kingdom expectation itself did not figure
prominently at Qumran, the community still had, as we have
seen, its own distinct version of eschatology. It conceived
of itself in eschatological terms, claiming to be the congregation of the end. Conversely, the strong imprint made by
the biblical twelve symbolism upon the overall structures of
the desert community is not comparable with the low profile
of the twelve concept imprinted upon the Christian traditions.
We have shown before that the earliest Christian references
to the twelve are not even supported by any first-hand knowledge of this alleged institution. Not even Paul knew the
twelve personally. If there ever was a group of 'the
twelve',[165] it was already in the earliest days of the church
so far removed from the scene that the witnesses could only
refer to them in second-hand fashion. Nonetheless, just as
the eschatological climate of the intertestamental age had a
strong effect on the Qumran covenanters, so also the well-
familiar biblical twelve symbolism commended itself to the
post-Easter community, inviting it to avail itself of the interpretive wealth of this number. No community can elude the
power of those ideas which, in its day, predominate over the
cultural or religious life of the people.

In this chapter, we have dealt with the significance of
the figure of twelve in the history of the Qumran community.
The covenanters envisioned the full restoration of Israel's
ancient twelve-tribe system at the end of temporal history.
In anticipation of God's future, bodies of twelve (priests
and laymen) were established, especially among the desert
branch of the brotherhood. The identification, however, of
the exact administrative function of these twelve-men bodies
is no less difficult for the Qumran sect than it is in early
Christianity. At Qumran they seem to have played an ideal

role rather than an actual one. While the actual authority
lay in the hands of a priest and guardian, the twelve men of
1QS apparently continued to remind the covenanters as corporate personalities of the brotherhood's imminent future.
In Israel's history, the idea of a perfect twelve-tribe confederacy was projected back, perhaps at the time of the united
monarchy, into the otherwise rather obscure beginnings of an
only loosely organized tribal union. Qumran projected the
very same idea into the future, anticipating the eschaton by
the appointment of otherwise relatively inert twelve-men bodies who had their place within the powerful Council. In both
cases the figure of twelve proved to be a most effective mode
of expression, suitable for the verbalization of the people's
religious consciousness. In Israel, the image of twelve
tribes, united in faith and acting in concert, whenever the
community's existence was at stake, resulted from Israel's
experience of Yahweh's continued guidance in its history. At
Qumran, the twelve members of the Council were the forerunners
of a new world, which persistently refused to come. Within
Qumran's contemporary power structure they do not seem to have
assumed any actual authority. One may conjecture that in the
community's actual life these duodecim did everything to get
out of the way of those who controlled the real life of the
eschatological desert brotherhood. Waiting, not acting, was
their 'office'.

CHAPTER II
THE EARLY CHRISTIAN 'NEW ISRAEL' SENTIMENT

All New Testament writers directly or indirectly advanced
the claim that the Christian community is the youthful
successor of the Israel of old. In his unusually brief
Galatian letter-ending, Paul calls upon the otherwise much
criticized Galatian churches, urging them to live by the
standard of his law-free gospel. All Gentile churches doing
so constitute what he calls 'the Israel of God' (Gal. 6:16).
Since the native Jew of Palestine by and large exhibited no
sympathy for Paul's gospel of free grace, the apostle la-
belled the Israelites sweepingly as 'enemies of God' (Rm.11:
28), cut off from their covenantal relationship into which
they had been born originally.

   To be sure, Paul's theological argument concerning the
old and the new Israel is rather complex, if not somewhat
confusing. In the apostle's view, Israel's sonship is next
to a _character indelebilis_. By virtue of God's irrevocable
election the Jews continue, Paul holds, to be the Lord's be-
loved people 'for the sake of their forefathers',[166] even
qua enemies of God. Paul's point here is that only for the
time being is Israel's sonship suspended. By a mysterious
act of God's grace, the apostle argues, the physical sons of
Abraham have voluntarily, yet only temporarily, vacated their
rightful place of sonship, so that Abraham's spiritual sons,
the Gentiles, would also be allotted a share in the blessings
promised to Abraham's seed.[167] Israel's 'enmity' to God
(_horribile dictu_) was for Paul merely a transitory stage in
the unfolding divine drama of salvation history. Ignoring
for a moment the immediate context of the Thessalonian writings, we might say that in Paul's theological judgment God's
holy will itself had brought his divine wrath upon the physical sons of Israel,[168] an act motivated solely by God's love
to those who could not claim to have come from Abraham's be-
getting. But what seems to be an inner-divine struggle

between God's love and his wrath was for Paul, in reality, only a salvation-historical sequence in God's divine economy. As he says in Romans, Israel's hardening of heart has come upon her only "until the full number of the Gentiles has come in" (Rm. 11:25). Once this has been accomplished, "all Israel will be saved" (Rm. 11:26), and Paul undoubtedly meant 'all' Israel!

The modern reader conversant with the history of Christian anti-Semitism cannot but take exception to Paul's ponderous argumentation. It must be said, however, that what is unacceptable to modern readers may have proven quite helpful to Paul's ancient audience. Some of Paul's references to the Jews, taken out of context, may indeed have aided and abetted the dark causes of medieval anti-Semitism. Yet such misuse of Paul's letters does not make the apostle himself into an anti-Semite. He was involved in an inner-Jewish controversy, pleading his case as a Christian Jew within what G. Vermes called "Jewry's rich intellectual creativity in the multi-party system of the pre-Destruction era."[169] For the apostle, the Gentiles' participation in the 'new Israel of God' was a first step in the direction of Israel's own return into its eternally valid covenantal relationship. The Gentiles are in Paul's perspective forever "in debt to the Jews" (Rm. 15:27), by reason that Israel had shared its most precious heritage with them. Only in this sense is the Gentile Christian community for Paul 'the new Israel'.

The new Israel concept of Q is not only less complex than that of the apostle Paul but also less cultivated and less refined. In the theological vision of the predominantly Hellenistic-Jewish Q scribes, the physical descendants of Abraham are all by and large comparable to what is called in the Document 'a rotten tree'. For Q, the sharp-edged axe of God's devastating future judgment is already laid to the root of the Synagogue's tree. The Synagogue is in the harsh judgment of Q no longer the community of God's future. The true Israel is composed solely of Jewish Christians of Q

provenance. Israel as a whole is written off en bloc, characterized as a tree to be cut down shortly and thrown into
the fire.[170]

Unlike Paul, the Q redactor(s) responsible for the compilation of the Document entertained no hope anymore for the
eventual restoration of Israel's 'sonship'. To be sure, the
Q scribes still called their fellow Jews to repentance but, as
A. D. Jacobson put it, "much of Q indicates that the mission
[to Israel had] been virtually abandoned."[171] The Q missionaries were no longer engaged in mission work proper but were
on what Jacobson rightly called 'an errand of judgment'.
"The 'Mission Charge' should not be understood as a 'mission'
at all but as an errand of judgment."[172] The Jews are invited here to leave Israel in order to join the ranks of the
'renewed' people of God, i.e., the Q community. Since the Q
Christians were of Jewish descent themselves, the designation
'new Israel' could not surface in the writings of this group.
Native Jews cannot speak of themselves as the 'new' Israel of
God. All they could do was to understand themselves as a
congregation of the 'renewed' people of God. Without ever
denouncing their Jewish heritage, they demonstrated at a late
stage of Q redaction their distance from Torah Judaism by
calling themselves "a group of 'babes' claiming special knowledge of the Father."[173] The program of radical obedience,
exercised by all the Q Christians as a necessary condition for
their membership in this group, suggested to them that they
were, in fact, the remnant community of which the prophets of
old had spoken so persuasively in various contexts.[174] As a
prophetic community, the Q group looked forward to the Last
Judgment, anticipating in its own peculiar kingdom proclamation the future role of being the 'twelve coassessors of
the Son of Man'.[175] In W. Schenk's recent reconstruction of
the Q order, the vision of the Son of Man judging the twelve
tribes of Israel in the presence of twelve Christian co-
judges (Mt. 19:28) par.) constitutes the concluding section
of the Q Document itself.[176] This final section of Q,

W. Schenk suggests, hammered home to the Q members how much
the Lord had entrusted into their keeping during the short
span between his death and his return as the Son of Man -
Judge (Mt. 25:14). Whatever the place of the passage may
have been within the hypothetical Document, Q indeed conceived of itself as the renewed Israel privileged soon to sit
in judgment over the unrepenting old tribes of Israel. To
put it differently, no single Q text unmistakably claims the
community to be the 'new Israel'. The underlying intention
of the Q redactor(s) nonetheless was to compose what A. Polag
rightly calls the constitution of the 'true Israel'.[177]

The pre-Markan twelve-disciple list, incorporated into
the Markan gospel by the evangelist himself,[178] is strong
evidence for the fact that the new Israel concept was not at
all foreign even to that strand of pre-synoptic Christianity.
Unfortunately, the theological hinterland in which this list
was originally created and in which it later circulated is
still densely covered with mist. But what else could the
twelve names have signified, if not the names of the twelve
patriarchs of the new people of God?

Matthew's new Israel concept is the Q sentiment re-
visited in the light of the sharp confrontation which raged,
in the post-Destruction era, between the Synagogue and the
Church.[179] We agree here with K. Holl who noted that Matthew's designation 'ἐκκλησία' represents the church as 'the
true Israel'.[180] Due to his own struggle with a self-conscious and freshly consolidated Judaism, the evangelist re-
inforced the harsh criticism of the Jewish religion which
characterized his sources. Matthew has indeed heightened
"the anti-Pharisaic tone of his sources," as G. D. Kilpatrick put it.[181] The earthly Jesus is in Matthew's gospel
a full-fledged Jew, ministering exclusively to the physical
sons of Abraham.[182] But Matthew made no secret of the fact
that Jesus' earthly ministry had failed to reach the ear of
the Jewish people. He was much too realistic to expect any
change in Judaism's future attitude to the messianic

proclamation of the church. He therefore dealt primarily with the Jews, excluding all Israel without the slightest hesitation from the blessings of the coming kingdom. We have shown elsewhere that the modern reader of the first gospel cannot avoid reading these tenets of Matthew's theology with feelings of uneasiness.[183] We do not need to reopen this debate in this context of our discussion. Suffice it to merely state that for the first evangelist the native 'sons of the vineyard' had irretrievably lost their former privileged position (Mt. 21:43). The Magi story (Mt. 2:1-12) summarizes well the evangelist's outlook on the Synagogue and its relationship to Gentile Christianity. The scriptural experts in Herod's vicinity (historically a misconception!) accurately point out to the Gentile astrologers visiting the palace on their way to the new-born king, the exact location of the Messiah's birthplace. In Matthew's perspective, the scribes and the Pharisees truly sit on Moses' seat, and are well informed of the secrets of Scripture (Mt.23: 2f). Yet they themselves fail to follow the lead of their own scriptural interpretation, leaving the search for the Messiah, and the drive to worship him, to the Gentiles and a handful of Jews such as Joseph, for instance, who was for Matthew an upright man of Davidic descent (Mt. 1:19f).[184]

It is in view of this that Matthew categorically declares that "the kingdom has been taken away from Israel and given over to the new people of God," i.e., the Gentiles, whom Matthew instructed to go one better than Judaism by repenting and producing the good fruits of the kingdom.[185] For Matthew, the Christian community is "the true end of Judaism" and all the wealth of Jewish life and teaching is focused on it.[186] In Matthew's theological judgment, the history of ancient Israel had come to its very end. In fulfillment of Isaiah's prophecy (Isa. 7:14), the 'Emmanuel' is now with the new Israel of Jewish-Gentile descent. Significantly, Jesus' promise to be with his followers 'to the very close of the age' (Mt. 28:20) is given on the mountain in 'the Galilee of the Gentiles'(Mt. 4: 15). All prerogatives of Israel have, in Matthew's gospel, been transferred to the new people of God, and to them alone.

Luke dwelt upon the same Q concept, although quite independently of Matthew. It has long been established that Luke did not have any solid knowledge of the minutiae of the Jewish religion.[187] In the third gospel, the Jews are depicted as being trammelled by prejudices against a messianic proclamation which they didn't wish to understand properly. In Acts, Luke presents the Jews as sinister troublemakers who almost for the fun of it chased Paul and his distinguished party from one place to the other.[188] By contrast, the church is in Luke's two compositions the salvation-historical replacement of the former people of God. The miraculous advance of the ever-extending and ever-growing ecclesia-community proved to Luke that salvation-historically a new era had dawned upon the world. Luke's Christian universalism, all-encompassing though it is otherwise, had yet no room for the renewal of the Jewish religion. No real place is assigned to Judaism in Luke's impressive overarching portrayal of redemption history, extending from Adam to the temporal end of the world. By implication, the book of Acts rather seems to concede that the otherwise highly successful church had lamentably failed to establish itself in the Jewish milieu in which it might have been expected to flourish as a Judaism with a faith and practice for Gentile godfearers.[189] Luke seems to know, to use G. Theissen's terms, that the Jesus movement had failed as a renewal movement within Judaism. "It found so little support that the Jewish historian Josephus could largely ignore it."[190] More often than not Luke's Holy Spirit therefore instructs the church to go everywhere, except to the Jews. The 'new Israel' of Lukan provenance turns away from its 'old' counterpart, and missionized only the Greek-speaking world. Admittedly, on their way to Greece and Rome, the Christian messengers encounter opposition from those Jews who had received their orders from the Jewish headquarters in Jerusalem (Acts 28:21). In terms of mission, however, Jerusalem is a lifeless and hopeless place. It seems that it had already disappeared from the map. The great

starting-point of all Christian mission is in Acts excluded
from the fruits of this mission: "Let it be known then . . .
that this salvation of God has been sent to the Gentiles; they
will listen" (Acts 28:28). Luke's Jews are a caricature. The
evangelist's so-called "fundamental anti-Jewish thesis"
(M. Dibelius)[191] is a device which highlights his notion that
henceforth the Christian church is to represent all the positive aspects of a religion which, by virtue of divine economy,
has at length been superseded.

Our brief review of the various new Israel concepts of the
New Testament cannot claim to have touched on all facets of
this all-pervasive Christian sentiment. Nonetheless, it should
be plain now that, quite similar to Qumran, the early Christian
community too conceived of itself in all stages of its theological development as the true congregation of the end of
days.[192] It is true, the specific designation of the church as
the 'new Israel' proper does not appear on the language level
of the New Testament.[193] But this is no proof against the presence of the concept itself. As we have seen before, in terms
of the church's consciousness, all New Testament writers universally agreed that the church is God's new/renewed laos, and
that as such it has replaced the Israel of old. The specific
term 'new Israel' is indeed absent from the New Testament. The
substance of the term, however, dominates in all the New Testament writings.[194] The religiously rich figure of twelve presented itself as a most effective hermeneutical vehicle for
bringing the New Testament's new Israel notion into focus. It
summed up most succinctly what the New Testament writers had
tried to say in their attempt to define the Christian identity
in its relationship to that of the Jewish community.

The number twelve was able to offer its services most
readily to the young Christian movement because the figure had
long since become what Norman Perrin has called a 'tensive symbol',[195] that is an expression flexible enough to represent and
accommodate the widest range of communal claims and beliefs as
well as the community's future hopes and its religious

expectations. All of these could not be expressed so perfectly
in any other fashion. Our investigation has shown that over
the centuries the zodiacal number had come to fulfill much more
than only one single role. It had long left behind the immediate company of purely mathematical magnitudes to become part of
the religious repertoire of the ancient communities. To borrow
M. Krieger's terms, the twelve had become a 'metaphor of window
opening' on the history of this number in the Orient and Occi-
dent, as well as a 'metaphor of mirror' on whose surface each
community could fathom the secret of its own identity.[196]
Ancient artists and scientists regarded the twelve as their number, although all of them on their own terms. The influence of
the twelve was not only confined to religious matters but rather
extended into the political, administrative and even architectural realm. And what is still more significant is that within
first-century Palestine and without, the figure of twelve was
in no need of any specific interpretation. It could take care
of itself, represent itself and speak for itself. Whenever and
wherever the twelve appeared, it unmistakably pointed beyond
itself, evoking the notions of sacredness, wholeness, unity,
divine presence and guidance, celestial glory and perfection.
The Christian community could not afford to pass over this number lightly. It suggested itself almost automatically to both
the early hermeneutes and the apologists of the Christian
faith. It is true, it was not the figure of twelve itself
which gave rise to the complex Christian new Israel consciousness. Christian identity has always resulted from personal or
community encounters with the risen Lord in the context of the
community's liturgy and worship,[197] and not from number speculations. But the number proved itself a most effective device
for the articulation of christological, ecclesiastical and eschatalogical dimensions latent in the Christian faith. At the
same time, the symbolic number challenged, through its very appearance in Christianity, the claims advanced by other religions, Jewish or Hellenistic. A few concluding comments are
called for about the hermeneutical power of the figure of the

twelve in the three early Christian concepts which we have
mentioned at the outset of this study.

In Paul's Corinthian correspondence, an unnamed group of
twelve witnesses is said to have seen the Lord. No specific
leadership role is assigned to them in the pre-Pauline confessional formula quoted by the apostle.[198] The twelve stand side
by side with other equally privileged individuals or groups of
witnesses such as 'the five hundred' and 'all the apostles'.[199]
The fact that the twelve appear in an early Christian formula
shows that they did not originate with Paul. However, although
the apostle had not created the twelve, he nonetheless manipu-
lated them hermeneutically by elevating them to a new level of
importance. These twelve men, originally said to have had an
appearance of the Lord, are used in 1 Cor. 15 to communicate
the soteriological purport of Christ's death and highlight the
historical factuality of the resurrection. The Lord's appearance to the twelve is presented by Paul as firm evidence for
the fact that 'Christ had died for our sins in accordance with
the scriptures and that he had been raised on the third day, in
keeping with the same scriptures' (1 Cor. 15:3-4). The group
of the post-Easter twelve, personally unknown to Paul, begins
to function here as the inalienable guarantors of the Christian
kerygma, investing it with historical respectability and authenticity. Paul's use of the twelve in this manner explains why
the twelve later became an integral part of the passion and
resurrection narratives, compositions both elaborating in story
language upon the concise kerygmatic content of Jesus' death
and resurrection.[200] Due to Paul's use of the twelve, the resurrection faith of the new people of God came to rest on twelve
irreplaceable pillars of truth. The Christian twelve replace
and offset here, by implication, the claims of the former
twelve-tribe community of Israel. What must not be overlooked,
however, is that 'the twelve' did not launch these far-reaching
claims themselves. As we have seen before, the pre-Pauline
formula had not elevated them at all to the rank of historical
guarantors of the kerygma. It was the apostle Paul who assigned

this role to the twelve. His conflict with Christians who
refuted his genuine apostleship made Paul activate an important
aspect implied in the symbolically rich concept of twelveness.
Paul surrounds these historically so mysterious twelve men with
the nimbus of 'founding fathers'. In claiming equal standing
with them, Paul conjured up, probably unintentionally, the
image of a qualitatively nuanced church authority. In the context of 1 Cor. 15, the twelve vouch for the resurrection as
first-rate witnesses, the authority of their testimony being
antecedently superior to that of all later witnesses. Ironi-
cally, in evoking this image, the apostle could not foresee
that decades later Luke, in another act of interpretation,
would boldly dwell on the inner logic of Paul's own assumptions
and subordinate even him to the powerful church authority of
the Jerusalem twelve. Paul himself thus had helped to raise
that group to the throne of first-rate resurrection witnesses
which in some later Christian writings would begin to eclipse
him quite appreciably.

The Q scribes did not portray the twelve as guarantors of
the Christian truth. In their vision, the twelve represent the
future. Q elevated its twelve to the rank of future coassessors of the coming Son of Man.[201] Whether as a symbolic representation of the community or as a specifically chosen body,
the Q twelve, presently inactive, are waiting 'in the wings'
to take their future action against the twelve tribes of
Israel.[202] Historically, the pre-Easter Q twelve are an even
more mysterious body than were already Paul's post-Easter
twelve. No evidence can be submitted in support of the argument that the Q twelve themselves, whoever they may have been,
had ever claimed to judge Israel as co-judges of the Son of
Man. It is the Q scribes who, sustained by their notion of
being the representatives of the renewed people of God, reactivated the eschatological implications of the multi-faceted
Jewish twelve idea. The representative role of the figure
twelve in the Qumran community is a striking, though independent, parallel to the Q usage of our number.[203] To lay stress

upon the historical authenticity of the Christian message did
not at all come to the mind of the Q hermeneutes. Their concern was to secure Jesus' earthly kingdom proclamation a firm
place within the life of the community. The Q scribes made use
of the twelve to point out that the Christian community has a
most promising future. Convinced of doing justice to the original intentions of the Torah, the Q duodecim (as a symbolic com-
munity-representation or an appointed body) expected to sit as
the delegates of the new Israel in the Great Hall of the heavenly Court of Justice, assisting the Son of Man in meting out
punishment. It is obvious that we encounter here another mean-
ingful application of the symbolic number to the Christian
tradition.

Unlike both the pre-Pauline and the Q twelve, the pre-
Markan twelve had neither a present nor a future function.
Twelve otherwise largely obscure figures appear in the pre-
Markan list by name. The pre-Markan community seems to have
asserted its own peculiar identity by availing itself of the
fundamental power inherent in the figure of the twelve. The
list seems to express the notion that the Christian community
is different from Judaism. The patriarchs of the Christian
congregation are no longer the sons of Jacob but rather a group
of newly appointed twelve individuals. Intent on writing a
christological gospel, the second evangelist did not really
know what to do with these twelve completely unknown figures.
Puzzled by their enigmatic names, Mark assigned the list to
what appeared to him the most logical place within the gospel.
He created missionaries out of them. These twelve men who, as
E. Best appositely stated, are 'typical believers' rather than
church officials,[204] do in Mark's gospel what all disciples
are commissioned to do: they preach the Word.[205]

No one should think that the pre-Markan name list must
represent actual names! The Magi tradition is a striking illustration of how easily in antiquity name-lists could be fab-
ricated. The nameless and numerically indistinct magi of the
pre-Matthean/Matthean tradition (Mt. 2:1-12) appear already

very early as the three royal figures of Balthasar, Melchior and
Gaspar (alias Hormizdah, Yazdegerd and Perozadh;[206] alias Hor,
Basanater and Karsudan). In some later lists of the eastern
churches they even have mysteriously grown into a group of
twelve fully named kings.[207] Name-giving has always been a de-
lightful act in life, not a difficult one! The pre-Markan list
is no exception to it. What we see here is that the church's
post-Easter claim to be the new Israel of God had been interpreted in foundational terms: according to the pre-Markan tradition, the new Israel has its own twelve founding fathers.
Mark then worked these twelve names into his gospel by retro-
jecting their symbolic role into the life of the pre-Easter
Jesus.

The common denominator of all three traditions is that
they bespeak the church's new Israel consciousness.[208] Paul's
twelve guarantors of the post-Easter kerygma function in Q as
the twelve eschatological judges of the renewed Israel, although temporarily without portfolio. These twelve figures
have been personified by the pre-Markan tradition. The twelve
names represent here the names of the twelve new patriarchs of
the new Israel. In the service of the church's new Israel
axiom, the historical, foundational and eschatological implications of the symbolic number have each been reactivated by
these three early Christian traditions.

It is worth mentioning in brief that these altogether di-
verse early Christian twelve concepts have evoked further speculations such as we find in Luke[209] and in the Book of Revelation. In the last book of the New Testament, the glorious
twelve have at length found their most distinguished resting
place inside the beautifully decorated walls of the heavenly
Jerusalem (Rev. 21:14). Even if the dependence of Rev. 21 upon
4QpIsa[210] should be denied, which is difficult to do, the Jewish parallels to Rev. 21 are so striking that uniqueness cannot be claimed for the Christian portrayal of the twelve as
honorary citizens of the Jerusalem above. In the Book of Revelation the post-Easter twelve, who had earlier appeared as

testes inter pares, have rather belatedly become the most distinguished dignitaries of celestial Jerusalem, a vivid illustration of the fact how readily in religion the last can become
the first to cross the finish-line.

CONCLUSION:

THE INTERPRETIVE POWER OF THE NUMBER TWELVE

We have tried to establish in this part of our study that the
religiously so attractive figure of twelve was a most suitable
vehicle for the verbalization of the eschatological claims
made by the early Christian community. Theological concerns
thus prompted the first appearance of the number in the New
Testament. This explains why it is not possible to trace back
convincingly any of the three early Christian twelve concepts
to Jesus' earthly ministry. The New Testament 'twelve' bespeak
the thinking of the post-Easter church, not that of Jesus
himself. It is true, the kingdom proclamation of the earthly
Jesus must have attracted odd numbers of more or less
loyal followers of Jesus. The complex Peter-tradition, for
instance, with all its ramifications is firm evidence in support
of the fact that the earthly Jesus had disciples in his entou-
rage.[211] However, what cannot be established by any tradition-
historical investigation into the source materials is that
Jesus ever had 'twelve' disciples around him, let alone that
he appointed them. Our point is that we do not even need to
establish this. As we have shown earlier, the twelve concepts
of the pre-Pauline/Pauline tradition, of the Q community and
of pre-Markan Christianity rehearse, each in different manner,
the post-Easter Christian 'knowledge' that Jesus' death and
resurrection marked a most decisive turning-point in (Israel's)
history. Epoch-making turning-points can never be identified
in terms of chronology, statistics or biography. As the
philosopher Hans Blumenberg has stated,

> The turn of eras is an elusive _limes_. It is tied to
> neither a precise date nor to any clearly identifiable
> event. It manifests itself to the informed observer
> as a kind of threshold which people either have not
> crossed yet or else to which they look back from a
> considerable distance.[212]

The Christ-event marks this type of watershed in history.
All Christian confessions, be they early or late, have tried
to respond to it in what may be termed a vision from behind.

The pre-Pauline church as well as the Q and the pre-Markan
communities have looked back to this event, and in doing so
availed themselves, among other communicative vehicles, of the
interpretive power of the symbolic number twelve. The figure
twelve is therefore part of the church's post-Easter confession
of Christ's Lordship. To trace the appointment of twelve
disciples back to a pre-Easter event in Jesus' ministry is in
view of this a rather futile exercise. The New Testament
references to Jesus' twelve disciples do not receive their
authority or verification from factual history. Who could
ever decide, for instance, whether Jesus appointed twelve
earthly missionary followers, twelve patriarchal figures or
twelve prospective eschatological co-judges of the Son of Man?
The power of the Christian confession is not bound to demon-
strable or neutrally observable facts. It is of a spiritual
nature. It is tempting to apply to the creation of 'the
twelve' Luther's definition of the difference between divine
and human love. Amor Dei non invenit sed creat suum diligibile;
amor hominis fit a suo diligibili (the love of God does not
find but creates the object of its love, whereas the love of
man is created by the object of its love).[213] The twelve were
created because they seemed to be the most suitable agents the
church could ever have in its attempt to illustrate the secret
of God's saving love to the world.

All ancient religious claims were claims to ultimacy.
Since the early Christian community was part of the ancient
world, it was unable to conceive of itself as merely participating with other religious groups in the religious quest of
the day. It insisted on being the only true people of God, as
all other religious communities did, with value-signs reversed.
Even Jewish Christianity itself, perhaps with the notable
exception of Paul, could not concede to orthodox Judaism a
continuing covenantal relationship with Yahweh. In antiquity,
the competing religions had not learned yet to compete in the
open space of mutual respect. As yet, the soil had not been
cultivated for inter-religious dialogue. Instead of submitting

religious claims existentially, they were advanced ontologi-
cally. The 'truth' of any one religion denied, by implication
and in a priori fashion, the truth-claim of all other religions.
The young Christian movement was from the outset under the
spell of this generally accepted mode of religious reasoning
and the New Testament records show it with greatest clarity.

Absolute claims run through the whole New Testament
literature. The Q group maintained that Jesus is qualitatively
greater than any other figure, whether it be John the Baptist,[214] Jonah or Solomon.[215] Matthew points out that Christian righteousness exceeds by far that of the Pharisees and
the scribes.[216] Paul argues that irrespective of Judaism's
scriptural expertise, a veil covers the mind of every Jew
reading the Hebrew Bible, the veil being removed only if and
when a Jew turns to Christ.[217] The Epistle to the Hebrews
reasoned in the same vein when it elevated Jesus to a rank of
glory far beyond that of Moses, or any angel for that matter.[218]
All these references show that the rapidly advancing and growing
early church was unable to content itself with the experience
of Christ's epiphany in its liturgy and worship. Like all
other ancient religions, it set itself up as the only true
representative of the divine.

The literary form of the story is the most widely used
vehicle by which the Christian community has advanced its
claim to the truth. Since 'narrative' has always a referent,
the Christian story advocated the beauty and power of the
Christian faith in popular missionary language. However, in
telling stories, the historically naive ancient Christian mind
confused the 'history-likeness' of the story (H. Frei) as a
literary genre with history itself.[219] The meaning of this
'history-likeness' was reduced to the meaning of the quasi-
historical events used in the story as modes of communication.
The narratives no longer 'narrated' the deeper concerns of the
Christian community. Divested of its missionary function the
particularities and peculiarities of the gospel narrative were
absolutized and began to represent objective history, a

function which they could not fulfill. Originally, the popular
Christian narrative, as conflict-, miracle- or illustrative
story, was to cast new light on the Christian confession of
Jesus Christ as Lord. The gospel story, however, appropriated
and monopolized the confessional claim itself, so that story-
telling was henceforth reduced to the reiteration of the first
gospel stories. The stories had become STORY; 'Geschichten'
had turned into 'Geschichte'. In Norman B. Petersen's terms,
the world represented by narratives became normative in themselves, the worlds of the narratives being confused here with
the real world, and interpreted in relation to it.[220]

The story about Jesus' appointment of twelve distinguished
disciples has rightly come to occupy a prominent place in and
among the early Christian narratives. Originally the story
contrasted the peculiar Christian self-consciousness with that
of Judaism, a self-consciousness resulting from the Church's
post-Easter experiences with Jesus, the Christ. In referring
to 'the twelve', early Christianity made use of ancient code-
language known to any ancient audience, Palestinian or
Hellenistic. In the course of Christian mission and expansion,
the elusive code-language became in itself a vehicle of interpretation, and gave birth to all sorts of twelve concepts,
eschatological and christological, earthly and heavenly. Once
twelve fully named patriarchal missionary judges had been born
into the Christian heritage, they began to write a history of
their own. They no longer merely illustrated the post-Easter
Christian consciousness but rather became a focus of truth in
themselves, proving the authenticity of the Christian faith
historically. Unaware of the sharp distinction between
'narration' (history-likeness) and 'history' (documented
historical events), the early church naively historicized
what originally had been vehicles of communication. Christianity now used its own stories to deny the right of any
further new story-telling independent of or unresponsive to
the canonized story. Christian story-telling was no longer
allowed to go past the officially approved story. Put

differently, the event narrated by the story of Jesus'
appointment of twelve disciples was estranged from the world
of stories to become part of 'sacred history', authenticating
sacred institutions rather than creating faith.

It speaks for the religious integrity of the three
earliest Christian traditions (not against them) that none of
them readily supports the historicizing tendencies of the later
church. None of the three differing traditions can be made
to affirm historically what, in essence, have been confessional
claims. In tracing them back to their origin, the church does
not come into the vicinity of the earthly Jesus or a divinely
warranted historical event. In working back from the gospels
to the earliest preshaped traditions, the church comes face to
face with its own identity, and is invited to either affirm or
challenge it. It is the mandate of historical-critical studies
within the context of confessional theology to enable each of
the early traditions to tell its own story, independently of
any other tradition, and in doing so to restore the joy of
narration. 'Narrated' claims must not be confused with
'historical' claims. Faith can move mountains but it cannot
convert the story about Jesus' appointment of exactly twelve
followers into historiography. The church is not apostolic
because the earthly Jesus himself has appointed just 'twelve'
earthly disciples. It is apostolic whenever and wherever as
a community representing 'twelveness' it is ready to confess
Jesus Christ, assuming responsibility 'with him' for an
imperiled world[221] in which the Lord has promised to be 'with
his followers' to the close of the age.

1. H. Guenther, "The 'Event' of the Resurrection," Shingaku
    Kenkyu, Theological Studies: Kwansei Gakuin, Vol. 18
    (1969), 1-36, 3-11.

2. Cf. Part I, fn. 95.

3. Cf. Part I, ch. III, 21-22, 30f.

4. Ibid.

5. Cf. Part I, ch. II, 13-19, especially fns. 58.59.

6. R. Bultmann, The History of the Synoptic Tradition, 341.
    Cf. Mk. 4:10, 6:7f. etc.

7. It is true, as E. Hatch stated, that Christian leaders
    "who have moulded the thoughts of their contemporaries,
    instead of being moulded by them, are always few in
    number and exceptional" (Edwin Hatch, The Influence of
    Greek Ideas and Usages upon the Christian Church, ed. by
    A. M. Fairbairn [Williams and Norgate, 1898], 10). What
    is important, however, is that exceptional leadership
    always leaves its traces behind, as we see in the Petrine
    and Pauline traditions. No discernible trace is left in
    the records by the twelve!

8. B. H. Streeter, The Four Gospels: A Study of Origins
    (London: Macmillan, 5th impr., 1936), 232.

9. G. Theissen, The First Followers of Jesus, 9. Also:
    "The group of twelve under [Peter's] leadership soon
    disappeared" (ibid.).

10. Charles H. Talbert, Luke and the Gnostics, 52, fn. 10..

11. Lk. 22:28-30/Mt. 19:28. Cf. Part I, ch. III, 23-25. The
    'Son of Man' title, used 30 times in Mt. (14 times in Mk.;
    25 times in Lk.), occupies an important place in Matthew's
    gospel. The designation denotes "a supernatural figure"
    (G. D. Kilpatrick, The Origins of the Gospel According to
    St. Matthew, 107).

12. G. Vermes, The Dead Sea Scrolls in English, 16. The
    members of the Qumran community expected the end of the
    world to come shortly (ibid. 53). They were determined
    to "remain in 'exile' until the Messianic war," and they
    hoped then "to reoccupy Jerusalem and conquer the world
    by defeating all the Gentiles..." (ibid. 61).

13. Cf. Part I, fns. 102.107. John's gospel will be left

aside in Part II of our study because it does not contribute anything to the clarification of the twelve
apostle tradition. Ch. H. Talbert's comment that John's
gospel makes "an appeal to apostolicity" introduces a
concept of 'apostolicity' which is misleading (Luke and
the Gnostics, 61). Cf. Part I, fn. 42.

14. Cf. Part I, Conclusion, 27-31.

15. R. McL. Wilson, Gnosis and the New Testament (Oxford:
    Basil Blackwell, 1968), 66.

16. Hippolyt, "The Refutation of All Heresies," in The Ante-
    Nicene Fathers, ed. A. Roberts/J. Donaldson (American
    Reprint of the Edinburgh Edition; Buffalo: Christian
    Literature Comp., 1886), Vol. V, 82 (Book VI, 18).

17. Ibid.

18. R. McL. Wilson, Gnosis and the New Testament, 76.

19. Ibid. It should be noted that in later gnostic systems,
    the twelve could even become a symbol of evil (cf. W. C.
    Grese, Corpus Hermeticum XIII and Early Christian Litera-
    ture, 19).

20. John M. Hull, Hellenistic Magic and the Synoptic Tradi-
    tion, Studies in Biblical Theology, Second Series 28
    (London: SCM Press, 1974), 1f.

21. Ibid. 42.

22. Chr. J. Scriba; with the assistance of M. E. Dormer Ellis,
    The Concept of Number (Mannheim/Zürich: Bibliographisches
    Institut (Hochschultaschenbücher Verlag), 1968), 137.

23. Cited by K. Menninger, Number Words and Number Symbols. A
    Cultural History of Numbers, tr. by Paul Broneer from rev.
    Germ. ed. (Cambridge, Ma.: The M.I.T. Press, 1969), title
    page.

24. In Greek culture, the talent had sixty minae (μναῖ).
    Whereas the Babylonian mina had sixty shekels, the Greeks
    established their own value table by equating the mina
    with one hundred drachmas (δραχμαί). One Greek drachme
    (δραχμή) equalled six obols (ὀβολός). Six thousand
    δραχμαί equalled one talent (τάλαντον) which, in turn,
    equalled thirty-six thousand ὀβολοί. It must be observed
    that, as K. Menninger states, "the talent and the mina
    were never issued by the Greeks as coins but were merely
    numerical measures..." (ibid. 162). Interestingly, in
    Lk. 19:11-27 "the servants operate with minas." The
    Matthean version of the Parable of the Talents (Mt. 25:

14-30) speaks of talents (G. D. Kilpatrick, The Origins of the Gospel According to St. Matthew, 125).

25. K. Menninger, Number Words and Number Symbols, 162.

26. R. de Vaux, "La Thèse de l'Amphictyonie Israélite," The Harvard Theological Review, Vol. 64 (1971), 415-436, 422f. Cf. Charles H. Talbert, What is a Gospel. The Genre of the Canonical Gospels (Philadelphia: Fortress Press, 1977): "Zeus determined that after performing the twelve labors, Hercules was to be given immortality" (29).

27. M. P. Nilsson, Geschichte der Griechischen Religion, Handbuch der Altertumswissenschaft, Bd. I (München: C. H. Beck'sche Verlagsbuchhandlung, 1967), 154 (Artemis 154/ Artimis 481?).

28. Ibid. 819.

29. Jacques-É. Ménard, L'Évangile de Verité. Nag Hammadi Studies, ed. by M. Krause et al. (Leiden: E. J. Brill, 1972), II, 27. G. D. Kilpatrick affirms the Jewish provenance of the first gospel. He nonetheless supports Jacques-É. Ménard by saying that what may at first sight appear more Jewish is not necessarily more original. We have to reckon with a "process ... of rejudaization and this rejudaization is quite distinct from the retention of original Jewish features" (Origins, 103).

30. Cf. G. Theissen, "Wanderradikalismus. Literatursoziologische Aspekte der Überlieferung von Worten Jesu im Urchristentum," ZThK, Vol. 70 (1973), 245-271.

31. K. Rudolph, "Simon--Magus oder Gnosticus," ThRs, NF, 42 Jahrgg (1971), 279-359, 285f.

32. E. Hatch, The Influence of Greek Ideas and Usages upon the Christian Church, 350.

33. Ibid. 4.

34. Ibid. 5.

35. R. M. Grant, Gnosticism. An Anthology (London: Collins, 1961), 26. B. H. Streeter suggests 225 C.E. as the date of composition for the Clementine Homilies (The Four Gospels, 258).

36. O. E. Neugebauer, "Zodaic," Encyclopedia Britannica, Vol. 23 (Chicago: W. Benton, 1971), 982.

37. Ibid.

38. The vernal equinox was changed from Capricornus (December 22-January 20) to Aries (March 21-April 20). By the same token, the autumnal equinox shifted from Gemini (May 21-June 21) to Virgo (August 24-September 23).

39. K. Menninger, Number Words and Number Symbols, 162.

40. F. Cumont, The Oriental Religions in Roman Paganism, 176.

41. Ibid. 178.

42. M. Noth, Das System der Zwölf Stämme Israels (Stuttgart: W. Kohlhammer, 1930), 86; N. K. Gottwald, The Tribes of Yahweh. A Sociology of the Religion of Liberated Israel, 1250-1050 B.C.E. (Maryknoll, N.Y.: Orbis Books, 1979), 366.

43. N. K. Gottwald, The Tribes of Yahweh, 345.

44. A. Bettelheim, "Twelve Tribes," The Universal Jewish Encyclopedia, Vol. 10 (New York: 1943), 330.

45. G. von Rad, Old Testament Theology: The Theology of Israel's Historical Traditions, tr. by D. M. G. Stalker (Edinburgh and London: Oliver and Boyd, 1962), I, 17.

46. M. Noth, Das System der Zwölf Stämme Israels, 62.

47. Ibid., 30-40.

48. The Deuteronomist pictured Israel's history as a history of disobedience. O. H. Steck (Israel und das gewaltsame Geschick der Propheten) observes that the concern of the deuteronomistic sketch of history was to come to terms theologically with the national disasters of 721 and 587 B.C.E. in the interest of providing a new basis for Israel's repentance and conversion (205-208). For further clarification of the concerns of the deuteronomistic history cf. H.W. Wolff, "The Kerygma of the Deuteronomic Historical Work," The Vitality of Old Testament Traditions by W. Brueggemann and H.W. Wolff (Atlanta: Knox, 1975), 83-100.

49. G. von Rad, Das erste Buch Mose, Das Alte Testament Deutsch, 2. Teilband (Göttingen: Vandenhoeck und Ruprecht, 1950), 55f.

50. N. K. Gottwald, The Tribes of Yahweh, 359.361.

51. Gen. 22:20-24; P-text.

52. Gen. 25:12.

53. Gen. 25:13-16; P-text.

54. G. von Rad, Das erste Buch Mose, Das Alte Testament Deutsch, 3. Teilband (Göttingen: Vandenhoeck und Ruprecht, 1952), 224.

55. Gen. 25:2.

56. The Edomites are regarded as being kin to Israel (cf. Dt. 23:7; Numb. 20:14; Amos 1:11).

57. Gen. 36:20-28.

58. G. von Rad, Das erste Buch Mose, Das Alte Testament Deutsch, 4. Teilband (Göttingen: Vandenhoeck und Ruprecht, 1953), 303.

59. Ibid. 302.

60. Numb. 1:5-15; 10:14-26; 13:4-15; cf. C. Westermann, Genesis, Bd. I/2: Biblischer Kommentar Altes Testament (Neukirchen-Vluyn: Neukirchener Verlag, 1981), 692.

61. N. K. Gottwald, The Tribes of Yahweh, 355; C. Westermann, Genesis, 686.

62. G. von Rad, Das erste Buch Mose, Das Alte Testament Deutsch, 2. Teilband, 55f.

63. N. K. Gottwald, The Tribes of Yahweh, 353.

64. C. Westermann argues that in the main the non-Israelite lists represent redactionally modified and expanded authentic (original) materials. Gen. 22:20-24 is for Westermann in its substance a genealogy of Abraham's extended family (Genesis, 451) which only later, due to the family's growth, was transferred to non-Israelite clans and tribes (449). Gen. 25:12-18 is not a genealogy at all (483) but a composite passage (v.12.17/13-16.18) (486), reproducing an old name list of Arabic tribes. In line with Gen. 12:3, these tribes are now said to have derived from Abraham (489). What was originally an old name list (Gen. 36:10-14) is in vv. 20-28 made over into a list of tribes (683). The source materials seem to have come from the royal archives of the united monarchy (684). The list of Gen. 36:9-14 (without Amalek v. 12) contains twelve (686), vv. 15-19 fourteen, vv. 40-43 eleven names. "The twelveness indicated in vv. 9-14 betokens totality" (686).

65. N. K. Gottwald, The Tribes of Yahweh, 354.

66. Ibid. 367.

67. Gen. 25:16.

68. N. K. Gottwald, The Tribes of Yahweh, 354.

69. N. K. Gottwald seems to be antecedently suspicious of all premonarchic references to twelveness. He regards them all as "suspect and perfectly intelligible as later editorial retrojections into the period" (361). He assumes that after the unification of the Israelite tribes in David's time an alleged 'traditionalist' (367.375), fascinated by the idea of Israel's twelveness, systematically inserted the twelvefold scheme even into those non-Israelite lists which had made no reference to twelveness originally. Old Testament scholarship has to provide much more detailed information on the person and work of this 'traditionalist' before this hypothesis becomes more tenable than the view that the lists, scattered all over the book of Genesis, retain premonarchic memories of non-Israelite clusters of twelve (six) tribe organizations. Gottwald's assumption that Israel may first have adopted the twelve tribe system for both administrative and religious purposes in David's (or possibly Saul's) time is as difficult to substantiate as is M. Noth's earlier reconstruction of a twelve tribe system on the analogy of the Greek amphictyonies.

70. Some exceptions to twelve-member coalitions have to be noted: the amphictyony around the Poseidon shrine at Calauria had reportedly only seven participating members; the Latin amphictyony on Mons Albanus was composed of thirty members, and the late Etruscan coalition had grown to a fifteen member association (cf. N. K. Gottwald, The Tribes of Yahweh, 353).

71. M. P. Nilsson, Geschichte der Griechischen Religion, 554.653.

72. M. Noth, Das System der Zwölf Stämme Israels, 48f.

73. R. de Vaux, "La Thèse de l'Amphictyonie Israélite," 419f.

74. F. Cumont, The Oriental Religions in Roman Paganism, 172.

75. The penchant of the biblical writers for the symbolic use of numbers had already been pointed out in the early days of the historical-critical investigation of the Old and New Testament (cf. H. J. Holtzmann, Die Synoptiker-Die Apostelgeschichte. Hand-Commentar zum Neuen Testament, Erster Band [2. verbesserte und vermehrte Auflage, Freiburg i.Br.: Akad. Verlagsbuchhandlung v. J. C. B. Mohr, 1892], 5). It is especially the seven which stands out sharply among the numbers preferred by the biblical authors. "The preference for the 'seven' runs in Matthew's blood," says J. Wellhausen in his Einleitung in die ersten drei Evangelien, 67. The same judgment holds

true for the writer of the book of Revelation. In
biblical thinking, the 'seven' is "the perfect number"
(R. E. Brown, The Birth of the Messiah, A Commentary on
the Infancy Narratives in Matthew and Luke, 75). The
seven derived its importance from the attention the
ancient astrologers used to pay to the seven planets.
The seven-day week seems to have been fashioned on the
same principle. The Qumran community displays an equally
strong liking for the 'seven'. The War Rule (1QM), for
instance, speaks of seven priests, seven Levites, seven
rams' horns, etc. (G. Vermes, The Dead Sea Scrolls in
English, 133). The Damascus Rule ordains that a man
healed from the error of profaning the Sabbath must be
kept in custody for seven years (ibid. 113f). The four
cardinal points invested the 'four' with symbolic significance (1 En. 22). The wind blows from the four firmly
established corners of the earth!

76. M. Noth, Das System der Zwölf Stämme Israels, 46.58; G.
     von Rad, Old Testament Theology, Vol. I, 17.

77. N. K. Gottwald, The Tribes of Yahweh, 386.

78. The Greek amphictyonic council of delegates and the rule
     to worship at one central shrine do not have counterparts
     in Israel's tribal system (cf. N. K. Gottwald, The Tribes
     of Yahweh, 376-386). "As to the existence of an inter-
     tribal body of delegates from the tribes which served as
     an amphictyonic council, there is absolutely no proof"
     (ibid. 350). Hence, "the peculiar traits of the Mediter-
     ranean amphictyony are not demonstrable in old Israel"
     (348).

79. R. de Vaux, "La Thèse de l'Amphictyonie Israélite," 436.

80. Ibid.

81. N. K. Gottwald, The Tribes of Yahweh, 374.

82. Ibid. 356.

83. Ibid. 374.

84. Ibid. 367.369.

85. Ibid. 363; details 366-382.

86. Ibid. 362.

87. Jos. 8:25; Jg. 21:10; 2 Sam. 10:6; 17:1; 1 K 10:26; 1 K
     19:19 (twelve yoke of oxen); Ps. 60.1f.

88. Cf. Part II, ch. I, 57-64.

89. Cf. Part I, especially 27-31.

90. The Qumran community, to which we owe the composition and preservation of the Dead Sea Scrolls, existed from ca. 140 B.C.E. to 70 C.E. (R. E. Brown, The Birth of the Messiah, 146). With the exception of the Temple Scroll, the scrolls were all found over a period of eleven years (1945-1956) in eleven caves on the northwestern shore of the Dead Sea. The Temple Scroll surfaced only in 1967 (cf. G. Vermes, "The Impact of the Dead Sea Scrolls on Jewish Studies During the Last Twenty-Five Years," Approaches to Ancient Judaism: Theory and Practice. Brown Judaic Studies I, ed. by W. S. Green [Missoula, Mont.: Scholars Press, 1978], 201-214, 202). Qumran literature, says G. Vermes, is evidence of "Palestinian Jewry's rich intellectual creativity in the multi-party system of the pre-Destruction era" (207).

91. G. Vermes, The Dead Sea Scrolls, Qumran in Perspective, 92f.

92. Th. H. Gaster, The Dead Sea Scriptures (Garden City, N.Y.: Doubleday, 1956), 3.

93. D. Flusser, "The Dead Sea Sect and Pre-Pauline Christianity," Scripta Hierosolymitana, ed. by Chaim Rabin and Yigael Yadin (Jerusalem: At the Magnes Press, Hebrew University, 1965), Vol. IV, 215-266, 265; G. Vermes, The Dead Sea Scrolls in English, 12f.

94. H. Jonas points out that "at the beginning of the Christian era and progressively throughout the two following centuries, the easter₁ Mediterranean was in profound spiritual ferment.... Palestine was seething with eschatological (i.e., salvational) movements and the emergence of the Christian sect was anything but an isolated incident" (The Gnostic Religion [Boston: Beacon Press, 1958], 31).

95. G. Vermes, The Dead Sea Scrolls, Qumran in Perspective, 117.

96. D. Flusser, "The Dead Sea Sect and Pre-Pauline Christianity," 218.

97. G. Vermes, The Dead Sea Scrolls in English, 16. It must be noted here that Qumran literature was written in Hebrew and Aramaic for the internal use of the community. No effort was made by the community to communicate its views to the Hellenistic world (G. Vermes, "The Impact of the Dead Sea Scrolls on Jewish Studies During the Last Twenty-Five Years," 208).

98. G. Vermes, <u>The Dead Sea Scrolls, Qumran in Perspective</u>, 128.130.

99. G. Vermes, <u>The Dead Sea Scrolls in English</u>, 14.

100. 2 Chr 18:18f; Isa. 6:1f. In his compilation, the Chronicler did not make use of the (proto-) Masoretic Hebrew text but rather used a text reflecting the Semitic substratum of the Greek Bible. This brings to light that in the history of the Hebrew Bible's translation into Greek "we have to reckon not with a single chain of tradition, but with a multiplicity of parallel sources" (G. Vermes, "The Impact of the Dead Sea Scrolls on Jewish Studies During the Last Twenty-Five Years," 206).

101. It is king Jehoshaphat of Judah himself who addresses the newly appointed judges in 2 Chr 19:5-8.

102. Ex. 28.

103. Ex. 28:1-4.9.11.

104. Ex. 28:15-30, especially Ex. 28:21.29-30; Lev. 8:8. The Urim and Thummin 'institution' seems to have been an oracle which was consulted in ancient Israel in times of emergency. According to J. M. Baumgarten, "the Urim and Thummin were viewed as one of the antique elements of the temple cult" yet "no longer accessible in the time of the Second Temple" ("The Duodecimal Courts of Qumran, Revelation and the Sanhedrin," 59-78). According to the Babylonian Talmud, confirmation by the Urim and Thummin was required for the expansion of the temple precincts (b. Shebuoth 2:2), for the declaration of war (b. Sanhedrin 16a). Further reasons for consultation are given by b. Berakhot 3b-4a and b. Yoma 71b. The Urim and Thummin, mentioned also in 1 Sam. 14:41-42; 28:6; Numb. 27:21; Ezra 2:63; Neh. 7:65; Dt. 33:8, are probably comparable to small pieces of wood with runic letters engraved on them. Cf. Joseph M. Baumgarten, <u>Studies in Qumran Law</u>. Vol. 24 of <u>Studies in Judaism in Late Antiquity</u> (Leiden: E. J. Brill, 1977), 145-171.

105. The War Rule (ch. VI) ordains "the horsemen [and their mounts shall wear breastplates] ... they shall all hold themselves prepared ... of God [ready] to spill the blood of the wicked" (G. Vermes, <u>The Dead Sea Scrolls in English</u>, 132).

106. Paul is frequently driven to speak of the temporary or even defective quality of the Law. In the apostle's view, the Torah and Christ seem to have been irreconcilable counterparts. The first evangelist does not

argue along Pauline lines. He may even have taken issue
with Paul, or at least a later Pauline position concerning the Law. It must be kept in mind, however, that
even Matthew claims Christ to be the giver of a 'revised' Law (G. D. Kilpatrick, Origins, 108.109.129).

107. The Hebrew text of the pesher has been made available
by D. Flusser, "The Pesher of Israel and the Twelve
Apostles," Eretz-Israel, E. L. Sukenik Memorial Volume,
Vol. 8. The translation submitted here is from J. M.
Baumgarten, "The Duodecimal Courts of Qumran, Revelation
and the Sanhedrin," 63.

108. J. M. Baumgarten, "The Duodecimal Courts of Qumran,
Revelation, and the Sanhedrin," 59.

109. Similar claims are made by the Q community (Mt. 19:28
par.). Cf. Part I, ch. III, 23-25.

110. The correspondence of images in the two writings is
striking. The pesher speaks of twelve priests and
twelve heads of tribes. The book of Revelation (ch. 21)
refers to twelve angels (21:12) and twelve apostles (21:
14). According to the pesher, God sits on a throne of
sapphires. In Revelation, the celestial Jerusalem is
bedecked with jewels (21:11). For the pesher, the glory
of the Urim and Thummin radiates into the eschatological
community. In Revelation, the radiance of the heavenly
city reflects the glory of God and thus is likened to a
rare jewel (21:11). The twelve priests of the pesher
are comparable to the twelve apostles of the book of
Revelation (21:14). Should all this be accidental? D.
Flusser's suggestion that Revelation made use of the
pesher by fashioning its Christian message after it has
much to commend itself ("The Pesher of Isaiah and the
Twelve Apostles," 52f). In following Flusser's lead,
J. M. Baumgarten focused his attention on the twelve
symbolism manifest in both writings. He comes to the
conclusion that "Revelation uses the twelve stones of
the Urim and Thummin as symbols for the apostles" ("The
Duodecimal Courts of Qumran, Revelation, and the Sanhedrin," 77). The correspondence of Rev. 21 and 4QpIsa
is for him "even closer than that indicated by Flusser"
(ibid.).

111. G. Vermes, The Dead Sea Scrolls, Qumran in Perspective,
106.

112. Ibid. 88-97.

113. G. Vermes, The Dead Sea Scrolls in English, 71-94.

114. G. Vermes suggests B.C.E. 150-110 as the date of composition of the Manual of Discipline (1QS) (ibid. 71).

115. G. Vermes, The Dead Sea Scrolls, Qumran in Perspective, 105.

116. Ibid. 130.

117. Ibid. 89; cf. G. Vermes, The Dead Sea Scrolls in English, 78-80.

118. G. Vermes, The Dead Sea Scrolls, Qumran in Perspective, 119.

119. G. Vermes calls the town sectaries 'the people of the covenant' or the 'camp sectaries' (ibid. 97.103.106.107. 129).

120. G. Vermes, The Dead Sea Scrolls in English, 95-117. B.C.E. 100 is the suggested date for the Damascus Rule (CD).

121. G. Vermes, The Dead Sea Scrolls, Qumran in Perspective, 105. The Rule strongly advises the members to aid one another in times of need.

122. Ibid. 97.

123. Ibid. 88.

124. The full members of the community claimed to be 'the sons of light'.

125. The Jewish religious establishment (orthodox Judaism), the Romans and the representatives of Hellenistic culture are for the Qumran brotherhood 'the sons of darkness'.

126. J. M. Baumgarten, "The Duodecimal Courts of Qumran, Revelation, and the Sanhedrin," 65.

127. The community's rigid initiation laws (cf. G. Vermes, The Dead Sea Scrolls, Qumran in Perspective, 93.95f.), the property laws as well as the rules about the community's common meal, attended only by members in good standing, are all determined by the group's eschatological expectations. It is not surprising that only fully fledged Jews were admitted into the desert fellowship (1QS, VI; cf. G. Vermes, The Dead Sea Scrolls in English, 81).

128. The number of twelve appears in 1QS VIII,1, a passage which speaks of "twelve men and three priests" (cf.

G. Vermes, The Dead Sea Scrolls in English, 85). It
also appears in 4QOrd 2-4; 3-4 where the reference is
to a "court of twelve," with two priests being included.
In 1QM 2:1 (G. Vermes, The Dead Sea Scrolls in English,
125) 'twelve priests' are mentioned. In 4Q159 (Ordinances), we hear of 'an advisory body of twelve' which
is modelled on Jehoshaphat's central tribunal (2 Chr 19:
5-11). For further discussion see J. M. Baumgarten,
"The Duodecimal Courts of Qumran, Revelation, and the
Sanhedrin," 59.

129. The dating of this document which lays down the basic
rules for the formation and advancement of the Holy Army
in the allegedly imminent eschatological war is rather
difficult. The appearance of references to the art of
war as practiced by the Roman legions suggests to G.
Vermes the last decades of the first century B.C.E. or
the beginning of the first century C.E. as the date of
composition (The Dead Sea Scrolls in English, 123).

130. In Qumran's perspective, the final adversaries were the
people of Kittim, i.e., the Romans, led by their king
(1QM,I.XI.XV.XVII; cf. G. Vermes, op. cit. 124.138.143.
146; also G. Vermes, The Dead Sea Scrolls, Qumran in
Perspective, 124). The time of this war has been
ordained by God: "Thou hast appointed the day of battle
from ancient times..." (1QM, XIII and XVII; cf. G.
Vermes, The Dead Sea Scrolls in English, 141.145).

131. 1QM, VII (G. Vermes, op. cit. 132).

132. 1QM, II, G. Vermes, op. cit. 126.

133. The reference is to Dan. 12:1 (cf. 1QM, XVII; G. Vermes,
op. cit. 145). In ch. IX of the War Rule we find listed
the archangels Michael, Gabriel, Raphael and Sariel
(G. Vermes, op. cit. 136). Sariel's history in the tradition is reviewed by G. Vermes, "The Impact of the Dead
Sea Scrolls on Jewish Studies During the Last Twenty-
Five Years," 212.

134. 1QM, III.V (cf. G. Vermes, The Dead Sea Scrolls in
English, 128.130).

135. 1QM, I,XVII (cf. G. Vermes, op. cit. 124.145).

136. The true Israel concept shows through in 1QM, XIII:
"Blessed be the God of Israel, for His holy purpose and
for His works of truth" (G. Vermes, op. cit. 140).

137. 1QM, II (G. Vermes, op. cit. 126).

138. 1QM, I (G. Vermes, op. cit. 124).

139. Ibid.

140. 1QM, II (G. Vermes, op. cit. 125).

141. Ibid.

142. 1QM, XVII (G. Vermes, op. cit. 146).

143. 1QM, XIX (G. Vermes, op. cit. 147f.).

144. 4QOrd. 2-4:3-4 cited in J.M. Baumgarten, "The Duodecimal Courts of Qumran, Revelation, and the Sanhedrin," 59.

145. "With the king shall be twelve chiefs of his people, and the priests twelve, and of the Levites twelve, who shall be sitting together with him (to counsel) concerning matters of law and Torah" (ibid. 59).

146. Ibid.

147. Cf. ibid. 78.

148. Cf. G. Bornkamm, Jesus of Nazareth, tr. by I. and F. McLusky (New York: Harper, 1960), 95; Ph. Vielhauer, "Speise und Trank Johannes des Täufers," in Aufsätze zum Neuen Testament (München: Chr. Kaiser Verlag, 1965), 47-54, 54; J. Gnilka, Das Evangelium nach Markus, Ev.-Kath. Kommentar zum Neuen Testament II/1 (Zürich: Benziger Verlag, 1978), 58; J.T. Milik concludes his discussion of 1 En. 83-90 by saying that "the final era will merely be a repetition, completely perfect in time, of the primordial era," J. T. Milik, The Books of Enoch: Aramaic Fragments of Qumran Cave 4 (Oxford: Clarendon Press, 1976), 45.

149. According to 1QS,V, the Priest was in control of the ritual (G. Vermes, The Dead Sea Scrolls in English, 79; cf. ibid. 20). Although we hear very little of the Priest (G. Vermes calls him a 'shadowy figure', cf. The Dead Sea Scrolls. Qumran in Perspective, 108), he nonetheless must have ranked first in the community (1QS, II; cf. G. Vermes, The Dead Sea Scrolls in English, 18.74).

150. G. Vermes, The Dead Sea Scrolls. Qumran in Perspective, 95.103.106.107. The Guardian is the mebaqqer or the maskil (ibid. 90,91), the so-called 'doresh ha-Torah'. "The Master shall instruct all the sons of light and shall teach them the nature of all the children of men according to the kind of spirit which they possess" (1QS, I.III; cf. G. Vermes, The Dead Sea Scrolls in English, 72.75).

151. The Bursar was the charge d'affaires, the mebaqqer 'al
melekheth ha-rabbim, concerned with the practical matters
of the administration and the finances (cf. G. Vermes,
op. cit. 20; G. Vermes, The Dead Sea Scrolls. Qumran in
Perspective, 90).

152. 1QS, VIII. Cf. G. Vermes, The Dead Sea Scrolls in
English, 85.

153. Ibid.

154. Ibid.

155. G. Vermes points out that the Habakkuk commentary (1QpHab),
for instance, "tacitly assumes that the Jerusalem temple
has lost its holy status and is superseded by the community's supreme institution, the Council, until the seventh
year of the eschatalogical war" (G. Vermes, "The Impact of
the Dead Sea Scrolls on Jewish Studies During the Last
Twenty-Five Years," 211).

156. G. Vermes leaves open the question of whether the twelve men
and the three priests "formed the nucleus of the sect as a
whole, or the minimum quorum of the sect's leadership symbolizing the twelve tribes and the three Levitical clans,
or a special elite within the Council...." (The Dead Sea
Scrolls. Qumran in Perspective, 91f.). J.M. Baumgarten
offers a solution. The designation 'Council', he suggests,
is frequently used "for the sect as a whole" but in 1QS,
VIII, 1 it is a term "for the select deliberative body ...
made up of priests and lay members" ("The Duodecimal
Courts of Qumran, Revelation, and the Sanhedrin," 63).
It is hardly accidental that in the otherwise so concrete
and detailed Serek ha-Yahad the exact role of these twelve
men continues to hang in a state of limbo. Their major
function seems to have been a representative one. They
represented proleptically what only the future could bring
to realization. The twelve council members of 1QS, VIII
kept alive the hope in the perfect restoration of Israel's
twelve tribe system. In the meantime, all current religious and administrative authority remained in the hands
of the Priest, the Guardian and the Bursar.

157. The community envisioned the appointment of a judicial
body in the renewed Jerusalem of the future. "The 'heads
of the tribes of Israel'," says J.M. Baumgarten with reference to 1QM and 4QpIsa, "belong to the realm of future
expectation, as does the king of the Temple Scroll" ("The
Duodecimal Courts of Qumran, Revelation, and the Sanhedrin,"
65, fn. 20).

158. G. Vermes, The Dead Sea Scrolls. Qumran in Perspective, 88.

159. CD X. Cf. G. Vermes, The Dead Sea Scrolls in English, 111.

160. G. Vermes, op. cit. 21.

161. Similar to the Book of Jubilees (ch. 33,2), the Damascus
     Rule (CD II.III; cf. G. Vermes, op cit. 98.99) instructs
     the community to 'keep the commandments' (i.e., the Deca-
     logue). "Qumran exegesis," says G. Vermes, "either pre-
     cedes Jubilees (as the Genesis Apocryphon may well do),
     or stands between this second century B.C.E. re-writing
     of the Genesis story and the midrash embedded in rabbinic
     literature" ("The Impact of the Dead Sea Scrolls on Jew-
     ish Studies During the Last Twenty-Five Years, 210).

162. D. Flusser, "The Dead Sea Sect in Pre-Pauline Christianity,"
     216.

163. G. Vermes, The Dead Sea Scrolls in English, 14. Whatever
     one may think of D. Flusser's contention that Jesus and
     his followers were "nearer to Pharisaic Judaism than to
     the Qumran Sect" ("The Dead Sea Sect and Pre-Pauline
     Christianity," 216), some sort of religious interaction
     between all the Palestinian groups can hardly be ruled
     out antecedently. "The number and importance of the no-
     tions ... common to the Dead Sea Scrolls and ... [early]
     Christianity mean that these points of contact cannot be
     explained away as incidental" (ibid. 263). G. Vermes af-
     firms these assumptions by saying that "the Scrolls have
     revealed themselves as a brilliant parallel to the New
     Testament attempt to defend beliefs by appealing to Old
     Testament oracles" ("The Impact of the Dead Sea Scrolls
     on Jewish Studies During the Last Twenty-Five Years," 210).
     D. Flusser's proposition, however, that Christian concepts
     such as the apostolate (cf. J.M. Baumgarten, "The Duo-
     decimal Courts of Qumran, Revelation, and the Sanhedrin,"
     77) "passed into Christianity directly from the Sect"
     (D. Flusser, op. cit. 265) is untenable.

164. A.D. Jacobson, Wisdom Christology in Q, 226.

165. 1 Cor. 15:5 (the Lord's appearance to 'the twelve')
     prompted E. Haenchen to suggest that 'the twelve'must
     have been more than a mere reflection of "the self-
     understanding of the Jewish-Christian congregation of
     Jerusalem" (Der Weg Jesu, 138). He thinks that 'the
     twelve' represented the Jerusalem community. It must
     still be noted that no records exist of their individual
     or group action(s). If there ever was a group of 'the
     twelve', their representative function must have been
     much less important than is generally supposed. So far
     as the early records go, they seem to have said or done
     nothing!

166. Rm. 9:4; 11:28.

167. 'The wild olive shoots' of Rm. 11:17 stand metaphorically for 'Gentiles'. Cf. Gen. 12:3.

168. "God's wrath has come upon the Jews at last" (1 Thess. 2:14-16).

169. G. Vermes, "The Impact of the Dead Sea Scrolls on Jewish Studies During the Last Twenty-Five Years," 207; cf. also Rm. 9:1-4.

170. Mt. 7:19 is apparently a reproduction of the Q saying Mt. 3:10/Lk. 3:9. In Mt. 7:19, the Baptist's anti-Pharisaic threat is made over into a Jesus saying of equal severity. Or should the invective against the Pharisees have been put into the mouth of the Baptist secondarily, as R. Bultmann seems to suggest (The History of the Synoptic Tradition, 117)? Already Chr. W. Weisse claimed that an original Jesus saying had been transformed here into a Baptist logion. Cf. Die evangelische Geschichte. Kritisch und philosophisch bearbeitet (Leipzig: Breitkopf und Härtel), 1838, II, 7.

171. A.D. Jacobson, Wisdom Christology in Q, 227. It must be noted that at all stages Q was "preoccupied with the mystery of Israel" (ibid. 226). However, the community's theological assessment of the Q mission changed considerably in the process of Q's consolidation.

172. Ibid. 134; cf. 133-144.

173. Ibid. 235.

174. 1 K 18:22; 19:18; 2 K 19:30; Isa. 1:9; Jer. 31:2; 50:2; Zeph. 3:12. In S. Schulz's terms, "the Q community is the eschatological community in Israel; obedience and observance of the charismatically intensified Moses Torah have salvific significance among the members in this time of the imminent end of history" (Q: Die Spruchquelle der Evangelisten, 350; my translation). Cf. A.D. Jacobson, "The Literary Unity of Q," 383f.

175. For a more detailed discussion of Mt. 19:28/Lk. 22:28-30 see Part I, ch. III, 23-25. The references to the judicial role of the twelve (either a community which understood itself symbolically as the new tribes of Israel or twelve individual delegates of this community) is the result of a lengthy development reaching back into the psalms. The pre-exilic (cultic-prophetic) Inthronization Psalm 82 (H.J. Kraus, Psalms. Bd. XV/2: Biblischer Kommentar Altes Testament [Neukirchen: Neukirchener Verlag, 1960], 570) takes over the originally Canaanite-Egyptian

image of God presiding at regularly held heavenly council gatherings. The members of this celestial עדה
(Götterrat) are called 'the sons of God' (Ps. 82:1; cf.
Ps. 58). It is interesting to note that even this heavenly Götterrat is upbraided for failing to uphold justice:
"You are gods, sons of the Most High, all of you; never-
theless, you shall die like men and fall like any prince"
(Ps. 82:6-7). In the perspective of this psalm, the
failure of the sons of God to judge the world with righteousness even put the stability of Creation in jeopardy
(ibid. 572). This process of subjecting the celestial
world to the judgment of God is continued in later Old
Testament literature. According to Isa. 24:21-23, God is
said to punish "the host of heaven" (v. 21). By contrast,
before the elders of Israel "he will manifest his glory"
(v. 23). Isa. 24 indicates that these elders now fulfill
the role formerly assigned to the heavenly sons of god.
This is in harmony with Dt. 32:8 where the celestial
'sons of god' (among whom God had originally taken his
place in the divine assembly as indicated by Ps. 82:1) are
identified with the (earthly) people of Israel. In the
later midrashim, these elders, frequently called now 'the
saints of Israel', are promised to "judge the world"
(Tanhuma, Shemot 29; Wisd. of Sol. 3:7-8; Dan. 7:22;
1 En. 1:9; 94f; 1QpHab 5:4f.). J.M. Baumgarten argues
that "in Mt. 19:28 the concept of the heavenly tribunal
emerges in a form which in substance is similar to that
found [in the midrashim]" ("The Duodecimal Courts of
Qumran, Revelation, and the Sanhedrin," 70). A similar
judicial function is exercised by the 'twelve chief priests'
of 4QpIsa. The appointment of the ten judges of the camp
covenanters (CD X) may constitute a further actualization
of these eschatological promises.

176. W. Schenk, Synopse zur Redenquelle der Evangelisten, 130;
cf. Part I, fn. 103.

177. "Man ist versucht, auf die Überzeugung der Redaktoren die
Überschrift 'Das wahre Israel' anzuwenden" (A. Polag, Die
Christologie der Logienquelle, 184).

178. Mk. 3:16-19; cf. Part I, ch. II, 13-15.

179. G.D. Kilpatrick, Origins, 101-123.

180. K. Holl, "Der Kirchenbegriff des Paulus in seinem Verhältnis zu dem der Urgemeinde," 45.

181. G.D. Kilpatrick, Origins, 36.

182. The significance of Jesus' ministry to the Jews is stressed
by passages such as Mt. 9:35f.; 10:5; 15:24. These texts,

taken together, highlight Matthew's conception that the earthly Jesus has ministered to the Jews only. In Matthew's reading, the Q text of Lk. 7:1-10/Mt. 8:5-13 strongly supported this facet of Jesus' ministry. According to Q, Jesus had not entered the house of the Gentile centurion. He rather had healed him from a distance.

183. H. Guenther, "The Negative Fascination of New Testament Language with Judaism," 28.29.35.

184. It should be noted here that Matthew was not the spokesman for orthodox Judaism. He was not intent on giving an objective description of Judaism's self-understanding. What Matthew may have had in mind is well put by R.E. Brown: "Jews who have the Scriptures and can plainly see what the prophets have said are not willing to worship the newborn king" (The Birth of the Messiah, 182). "Even though they can read the Scriptures correctly, they do not choose to believe" (ibid. 186). "In Matthew's mind, Jews who are true to the Law and the Prophets [such as Joseph] stand alongside the Gentile magi in accepting Jesus, while the authorities reject him" (ibid. 214).

185. Mt. 21:42-43; cf. G. Bornkamm, "End-Expectation and Church in Matthew," 43.

186. G.D. Kilpatrick, Origins, 122.

187. H. Guenther, "The Negative Fascination of New Testament Language with Judaism," 54-55.

188. Ibid. 52-62.

189. Cf. G.S. Sloyan, Is Christ the End of the Law? (Philadelphia: Westminster Press, 1978), 9.

190. G. Theissen, The First Followers of Jesus, 112.

191. M. Dibelius, Studies in the Acts of the Apostles, 8.

192. R. Bultmann, Theology of the New Testament (New York: Chr. Scribner's Sons, 1951), I, 37.

193. G.S. Sloyan, Is Christ the End of the Law?, 58.

194. Christianity began as a renewal movement within Judaism. Evidence of this abounds in the early strata of Q (Lk. 6:20-21; 6:37f.; 11:39.46; 16:17 par. etc.) - cf. A.D. Jacobson, Wisdom Christology in Q, 226f. - and the Pauline writings (Rm. 9-11 etc.). Like all other Jewish renewal movements (Qumran, zealots, Pharisees etc.), the early

Christian reform movement "wanted to make the better Israel a reality" (G. Theissen, The First Followers of Jesus, 85). It is true that the success of Gentile mission and the experience of history running undisturbed on its course prompted a loss of both eschatology (cf. U. Luz, "Das Jesusbild der vormarkinischen Tradition," in Jesus Christus in Historie und Theologie, Neutestamentliche Festschrift für Hans Conzelmann, ed. by Georg Strecker [Tübingen: J.C.B. Mohr (Paul Siebeck), 1975], 347-374, especially 352-359) and interest in Israel's salvation historical role (Lk. 10:21f.; 13:28-29.34f.; 14:15-24 etc.). But even then the theological problem of the relation of the Gentile community to Israel continued to occupy the mind of the church (Acts 7; Mk. 12: 1f.; Barn. 5 etc.). The continued reflection on Israel demonstrates the strength of the church's 'new Israel' sentiment, as well as its gradual spiritualization.

195. N. Perrin, Jesus and the Language of the Kingdom. Symbol and Metaphor in New Testament Interpretation (Philadelphia: Fortress Press, 1976), 30.

196. M. Krieger, A Window to Criticism (Princeton: Princeton University Press, 1964), cit. by N.R. Petersen, Literary Criticism for New Testament Critics (Philadelphia: Fortress Press, 1978), 24.

197. The Lord's encounter with Cephas (Peter) is personal in nature. By contrast, the appearance 'to all the apostles' and 'to the five hundred brethren' is a community experience.

198. Cf. Part I, ch. III, especially fn. 95.

199. 1 Cor. 15:6-7.

200. N.R. Petersen, Literary Criticism for New Testament Critics, 13. It is worth noting that the pre-Pauline formula (1 Cor. 15:3f.) established a logical sequence of the Christ-event along confessional lines: Christ died; he was buried; he rose and was seen. Mark replaced it with a narrative sequence corroborating the resurrection through the demonstration of the empty tomb (cf. the helpful comments of K. Baltzer, E. Brandenburger and F. Merkel, "Mk. 16:1-8," Göttinger Predigtmeditationen 27 [1972/73], 207). It is indeed enlightening to see that Mark explains "the resurrection kerygma in the form of a legend about women at the tomb" (U. Luz, "Das Jesusbild der vormarkinischen Tradition," 358). The evangelist seems to follow here the lead of the pre-Markan tradition which had consistently replaced, as U. Luz has persuasively shown, the eschatological orientation of the inherited tradition

with explicit references to the kerygmatized earthly Jesus
and his role in initiating and strengthening the community's faith in him (373).

201. Mt. 19:28/Lk. 22:28-30.

202. Cf. Part I, ch. III, 23-25.29f.

203. Cf. Part II, ch. I, 75-86.

204. E. Best, The Temptation and the Passion: The Markan
     Soteriology, 178.

205. Cf. Part I, ch. II, 13-15. As missionary-preachers the
     twelve were for Mark the representatives of the new com-
     munity, i.e., the representatives of the new Israel
     (E. Best, The Temptation and the Passion: The Markan
     Soteriology, 117).

206. Hormizdah, king of Persia; Yazdegerd, king of Saba;
     Perozadh, king of Sheba.

207. R.E. Brown, The Birth of the Messiah, 198.

208. Cf. Part I, fn. 77.

209. Cf. Part I, ch. I, 5-7.

210. Cf. Part II, ch. I, fn. 110.

211. The twelve-disciple list of Mk. 3:16-19, which Mark had
     found in his traditional material, inspired the second
     evangelist to create the idea of the twelve as Jesus' con-
     stant earthly companions (cf. Part I, ch. II, 13-16; ch. III,
     21). Once this idea had been created, it took on its
     own independent life, as we see from Luke's evaluation of
     the twelve to the rank of twelve apostolic eyewitnesses
     (ibid. ch. I, 5-7). While the references to twelve mis-
     sionary-preachers are of Markan making (for Mark, the
     twelve are essentially "typical believers," not church
     officials (E. Best, The Temptation and the Passion: The
     Markan Soteriology, 178), the mention of individual dis-
     ciples definitely precedes Mark. Some names are firmly
     rooted in the pre-Markan strands of the tradition (Mk. 1:
     16f.29; 2:14; 5:37; 9:2f.38f.; 10:35f; 14:33). The ab-
     sence of names from other pre-Markan units (Mk. 1:40f.;
     2:1f.; 3:1f.; 7:24f.) warns us against treating the former
     references as historical reminiscences per se (cf.
     R. Bultmann, The History of the Synoptic Tradition, 343.
     345). Nonetheless, the appearance of names in the earliest
     written traditions of the church still suggests strongly
     that disciples must have accompanied Jesus during his

earthly ministry. The name-change from Simon (Peter's pre-Easter name) to Cephas-Peter (a post-Easter designation) further supports this assumption. It is true that each synoptic writer gave the story of the name-change his own place (Mk. 3:16 - the calling of the twelve; Mt. 16: 17-19 - Simon's christological confession; Lk. 6:14 is Luke's reproduction of Mk. 3:16; Lk. 5:10 and Lk. 22:31, however, suggest another setting; the Johannine story about the miraculous draught of fish (Jn. 21:1-14) does not refer directly to Simon's new name. It still highlights his new commission which is elsewhere related to the name-change). But the variety of these independent traditions, plus the Lord's appearance to Cephas in 1 Cor. 15:5, suggests Simon's pre-Easter role.

212. "Die Epochenwende ist ein unmerklicher Limes, an kein prägnantes Datum oder Ereignis evident gebunden. Aber in einer differentiellen Betrachtung markiert sich eine Schwelle, die als entweder noch nicht erreichte oder schon überschrittene ermittelt werden kann" (H. Blumenberg, cit. in S. Schelz, "Umkehr am Rande des Abgrunds," Lutherische Monatshefte 19. Jahrgg. [1980], 634-637, 636; translation mine).

213. M. Luther, Conclusio XXVIII: Disputatio Heidelbergae Habita, in Martin Luthers Werke. Kritische Gesamtausgabe (Weimar: H. Böhlau, 1883), I, 365 (emphasis mine); J. Atkinson, ed. and transl., Luther: Early Theological Works, in The Library of Christian Classics (Philadelphia: Westminster Press, 1962), 278 (emphasis mine).

214. Lk. 7:28b/Mt. 11:11b. Most probably, this text represents a later addition to Q (A.D. Jacobson assigns it to the intermediate redactional stage; cf. Wisdom Christology in Q, 94). Notwithstanding its overall Markan dependence, Lk. 3:16/Mt. 3:11 has also been claimed as a Q text by most Q scholars (S. Schulz, Q: Die Spruchquelle der Evangelisten, 366-378, assigns it to the Hellenistic-Jewish strata of Q; A.D. Jacobson, Wisdom Christology in Q, regards it as a later addition to Lk. 3:7-9/Mt. 3:7-10, 32f. 94; A. Polag, Die Christologie der Logienquelle, assigns Lk. 3:16-17/Mt. 3:11-12 to the late redaction of Q, together with Lk. 3:7-9/Mt. 3:7-10. But Lk. 3:7-9 par. challenges Israel's sense of security in her salvation [one of Polag's criteria for identifying late redaction, 16] as strongly as Lk. 13:28f.34f. It is not clear why the latter texts are assigned to the Hauptsammlung, 13.92f., while Lk. 3:7-9 par. is supposed to be late redaction, 15). Whether the Q Source opened with the proclamation

of John the Baptist (cautiously, S. Schulz, Q: Die Spruchquelle der Evangelisten, 369, fn. 311; affirmatively, W.
Schenk, Synopse zur Redenquelle der Evangelisten, 5) or
with the Beatitudes (D. Lührmann, Die Redaktion der Logien
quelle, 56) need not be discussed here. H. Tödt (The Son
of Man in the Synoptic Tradition) seeks to reconcile both
positions: "Except for the Baptist's preaching and the
temptation, Q begins with the Beatitudes" (270).

215.   Lk. 11:31-32/Mt. 12:41-42. A.D. Jacobson draws attention
       to Q's ambiguity about Jesus' status, a trait affirming
       the important role of Wisdom christology in the Document.
       Q expresses "the superiority of Jesus in quantitative
       rather than qualitative terms" (Wisdom Christology in Q,
       230). Although Wisdom has sent more than one messenger,
       Jesus is still the greatest among them. For further discus-
       sion of this point see A.D. Jacobson, "The Literary Unity
       of Q," 377, especially fn. 54.

217.   2 Cor. 3:15-16.

218.   Hebr. 1:4f; 3:3.

219.   H. Frei, The Eclipse of Biblical Narrative. A Study in
       Eighteenth and Nineteenth Century Hermeneutics (New Haven,
       Conn.: Yale University Press, 1974), 1-16, 103, 118 etc.

220.   N.R. Petersen, Literary Criticism for New Testament
       Critics, 38.

221.   The integrity of the church is challenged today by fre-
       quently religiously disguised hate-ideologies such as
       anti-Semitism, anti-Marxism, or outright racism. Mean-
       ingful contemporary story-telling could venture on re-
       activating the fact that Jesus had appointed 'twelve Jews'
       to be with him (Mk. 3:14). This interpretation of the
       account would help to speak against any form of disguised
       Christian anti-Semitism.

BIBILIOGRAPHY

Aland, Kurt, ed. Vollständige Konkordanz zum Griechischen
    Neuen Testament, Berlin, New York: W. de Gruyter, 1975.

Apostolic Fathers. The Apostolic Fathers with an English
    Translation by Kirsopp Lake, Vol. I, London: W. Heinemann,
    1912, reprinted 1965. (The Loeb Classical Library).

Atkinson, James, ed. and trans. Luther: Early Theological
    Works, Philadelphia: Westminster Press, 1962, (The
    Library of Christian Classics).

Baltzer, K.; Brandenburger, E.; and Merkel, F. "Mark 16:1-8,"
    Göttinger Predigt-Meditationen 27 (1972/73), 205-209.

Bammel, Ernst. "Herkunft und Funktion der Traditionselemente
    in 1 Kor. 15:1-11," Theologische Zeitschrift 11 (1955),
    401-419.

Barrett, Charles K. Luke the Historian in Recent Study,
    London: Epworth Press, 1961.

--------. "Shaliah and Apostle," Donum Gentilicium: New
    Testament Studies in Honour of David Daube, edited by
    E. Bammel, C. K. Barrett and W. D. Davies. Oxford:
    Clarendon, 1978.

Baumgarten, Joseph. "The Duodecimal Courts of Qumran, Revela-
    tion and the Sanhedrin," Journal of Biblical Literature
    95 (1976), 59-78.

--------. Studies in Qumran Law, Vol. 24 of Studies in
    Judaism in Late Antiquity. Leiden: E. J. Brill, 1977.

Best, Ernest. The Temptation and the Passion: The Markan
    Soteriology. Cambridge: At the University Press, 1965.

--------. "Mark's Use of the Twelve," Zeitschrift für die·
    Neutestamentliche Wissenschaft 69 (1978), 11-35.

Bettelheim, Anna. "Twelve Tribes," Vol. 10 of The Universal
    Jewish Encyclopedia. New York: Universal Jewish Encyclo-
    pedia, 1943, 330.

Bornkamm, Günther. Jesus of Nazareth. Translated by I. and
    F. McLuskey. New York: Harper, 1960.

Bornkamm, Günther; Barth, Gerhard; and Held, Hans Joachim.
    Tradition and Interpretation in Matthew. Translated by
    Percy Scott. London: SCM Press, 1963 (New Testament
    Library).

Brown, Raymond E. The Birth of the Messiah: A Commentary on the Infancy Narratives in Matthew and Luke. New York: Doubleday, 1977.

Bultmann, Rudolf. The History of the Synoptic Tradition, Translated by J. Marsh, New York: Harper & Row, 1963. (Translated from the second German edition, 1931; second English edition, revised, 1968).

Conzelmann, Hans. "Luke's Place in the Development of Early Christianity," Studies in Luke-Acts, ed. by L. E. Keck/ J. L. Martyn. Nashville: Abingdon Press, 1966, 298-316.

--------. History of Primitive Christianity. Translated by John E. Steely. Nashville: Abingdon Press, 1973.

Cumont, Franz. The Oriental Religions in Roman Paganism. Chicago: Open Court Publication Company, 1911.

Dibelius, Martin. From Tradition to Gospel. Translated by Bertram L. Woolf. New York: Charles Scribner's Sons, 1935.

--------. Studies in the Acts of the Apostles. Edited by Heinrich Greeven. Translated by Mary Ling. London: SCM Press, 1956.

Edwards, Richard A. A Theology of Q: Eschatology, Prophecy, and Wisdom. Philadelphia: Fortress Press, 1976.

Ehrhardt, Arnold. The Apostolic Succession in the First Two Centuries of the Church. London: Lutterworth Press, 1953.

Farmer, William R. The Synoptic Problem: A Critical Analysis. New York: Macmillan, 1964.

Farrer, Austin M. "On Dispensing with Q," in Studies in the Gospels. Edited by Dennis E. Nineham. Oxford: Blackwell, 1955.

Flusser, David G. "The Dead Sea Sect and Pre-Pauline Christianity," Vol. IV of Scripta Hierosolymitana, edited by Chaim Rabin and Yigael Yadin. Jerusalem: At the Magnes Press, Hebrew University, 1965, 215-266.

--------. "The Pesher of Isaiah and the Twelve Apostles," Vol. 8 of E. L. Sukenik Memorial Volume, Eretz-Israel. Jerusalem: Israel Exploration Society, 1967, 52-62.

Frei, Hans. The Eclipse of Biblical Narrative. A Study in Eighteenth and Nineteenth Century Hermeneutics. New Haven, Conn.: Yale University Press, 1974.

Fridrichsen, Anton, "The Apostle and His Message," Uppsala Universitets Arsskrift 1947, 2-23.

Fuller, Reginald H. The Formation of the Resurrection Narratives. New York: Macmillan, 1971.

Gärtner, Bertil E. Iscariot. Translated by Victor I. Gruhn. No. 29 of Biblical Series. Facet Books. Philadelphia: Fortress Press, 1971.

Gaster, Theodor H., ed. and trans. The Dead Sea Scriptures: in English Translation. Garden City, N.Y.: Doubleday, 1956.

Gnilka, Joachim. Das Evangelium nach Markus. Bd. II/1: Evangelisch-Katholischer Kommentar zum Neuen Testament. Zürich: Benziger Verlag, 1978.

Gottwald, Norman K. The Tribes of Yahweh. A Sociology of the Religion of Liberated Israel: 1250-1050 B. C. E. Maryknoll, N.Y.: Orbis Books, 1979.

Grant, Robert M., ed. Gnosticism. An Anthology. London: Collins, 1961.

Grese, William C. Corpus Hermeticum XIII and Early Christian Literature. Vol. 5 of Studia ad Corpus Hermeticum Novi Testamenti. Leiden: E. J. Brill, 1979.

Guenther, Heinz. "The 'Event' of the Resurrection," Shingaku Kenkyu, Theological Studies: Kwansei Gakuin 18 (1969), 1-36.

--------. "The Negative Fascination of New Testament Language with Judaism," Shingaku Kenkyu, Theological Studies: Kwansei Gakuin 31 (1983), 23-75.

Haenchen, Ernst. "Matthäus 23," in Gott und Mensch: Gesammelte Aufsätze. Tübingen: J.C.B. Mohr (P. Siebeck),1965, 29-54.

--------. Der Weg Jesu: Eine Erklärung des Markusevangeliums und der Kanonischen Parallelen. Berlin: Töpelmann, 1966.

--------. The Acts of the Apostles: A Commentary. Translated by B. Noble and G. Shinn et al. Philadelphia: Westminster Press, 1971.

Harnack, Adolf von. New Testament Studies II. The Sayings of Jesus: The Second Source of St. Matthew and St. Luke. Translated by J. R. Wilkinson. London: Williams & Norgate, 1908.

--------. "Die Verklärungsgeschichte Jesu, der Bericht des Paulus (1 Kor. 15:3f) und die beiden Christus-Visionen des Petrus," Sitzungsberichte der Preussischen Akademie der Wissenschaften. Berlin, 1922, 62-80.

Hatch, Edwin. The Influence of Greek Ideas and Usages upon the Christian Church. Edited by A. M. Fairbairn; 7th edition. London: Williams and Norgate, 1898. (Hibbert Lectures, 1888).

Hippolyt. The Refutation of all Heresies. Vol V. of The Ante-Nicene Fathers, edited by A. Roberts and J. Donaldson. American Reprint of the Edinburgh Edition. Buffalo: Christian Literature Company, 1886.

Hoffmann, Paul. Studien zur Theologie der Logienquelle. Neue Serie No. 8: Neutestamentliche Abhandlungen. Münster: Aschendorff, 1972.

Holl, Karl. "Der Kirchenbegriff des Paulus in seinem Verhält- nis zu dem der Urgemeinde: 1921," Gesammelte Aufsätze zur Kirchengeschichte. Band II: Der Osten. Darmstadt: Wissenschaftliche Buchgesellschaft, 1964, 44-67.

Holtzmann, Heinrich Julius. Die Synoptischen Evangelien: Ihr Ursprung und Geschichtlicher Character. Leipzig: W. Engelmann, 1863.

--------. Die Synoptiker-Die Apostelgeschichte. Bd. I: Hand- Commentar zum Neuen Testament. 2. verbesserte und vermehrte Auflage. Freiburg i. Br.: Akademische Verlags- buchhandlung von J. C. B. Mohr, 1892.

--------, Lehrbuch der Historisch-Kritischen Einleitung in das Neue Testament. 3. Aufl. Freiburg i. Br.: J. C. B. Mohr (P. Siebeck), 1892.

Hull, John M. Hellenistic Magic and the Synoptic Tradition. No. 28 of Second Series: Studies in Biblical Theology. London: SCM Press, 1974.

Jacobson, Arland D. Wisdom Christology in Q. Ph.D. Disserta- tion, Claremont Graduate School. 1978. (University Microfilms International).

--------. "The Literary Unity of Q," Journal of Biblical Literature 101 (1982), 365-389.

Jonas, Hans. The Gnostic Religion. Boston: Beacon Press, 1958.

Käsemann, Ernst. "The Disciples of John the Baptist in Ephesus," Essays on New Testament Themes. Translated by W. J. Mon- tague. London: SCM Press, 1964, 136-148. (Studies in Biblical Theology Series).

--------. "The Structure and Purpose of the Prologue to John's Gospel," New Testment Questions of Today. Translated by W. J. Montague. London: SCM Press, 1969, 138-167.

Kee, Howard C. *Jesus in History: An Approach to the Study of the Gospels*. New York: Harcourt, Brace & World, 1970.

Kelber, Werner H. "The Hour of the Son of Man and the Temptation of the Disciples," in *The Passion in Mark. Studies on Mark 14-16*, edited by W. H. Kelber. Philadelphia: Fortress Press, 1976, 41-60.

--------. "From Passion Narrative to Gospel," in *The Passion in Mark. Studies on Mark 14-16*, edited by W. H. Kelber. Philadelphia: Fortress Press, 1976, 153-180.

Kilpatrick, George D. *The Origins of the Gospel According to St. Matthew*. Oxford: At the Clarendon Press, 1946.

Kingsbury, Jack D. "The Figure of Peter in Matthew's Gospel as a Theological Problem," *Journal of Biblical Literature* 98 (1979), 67-83.

Klein, Günter. *Die Zwölf Apostel: Ursprung und Gestalt einer Idee*. Göttingen: Vandenhoeck & Ruprecht, 1961.

Knox, John. *Marcion and the New Testament: An Essay in the Early History of the Canon*. Chicago: University of Chicago Press, 1942.

Kraus, Hans-Joachim. *Psalms*. Bd. XV/2: *Biblischer Kommentar Altes Testament*. Neukirchen-Vluyn: Neukirchener Verlag, 1960.

Lake, Kirsopp. "Note VI: The Twelve and the Apostles," in *The Beginnings of Christianity: Part I. The Acts of the Apostles*. Edited by F. J. Foakes Jackson and Kirsopp Lake. London: Macmillan, 1933. (Vol. V with additional notes to Commentary, ed. by Kirsopp Lake and Henry J. Cadbury), 37-59.

Lightfoot, Joseph B. *Saint Paul's Epistle to the Galatians*. 8th edition, revised text. London: Macmillan, 1884.

Lüdemann, Gerd. "Zum Antipaulinismus im frühen Christentum," *Evangelische Theologie* 40 (1980), 437-455.

Lührmann, Dieter. *Die Redaktion der Logienquelle*. No. 33: *Wissenschaftliche Monographien zum Alten und Neuen Testament*. Neukirchen-Vluyn: Neukirchener Verlag, 1969.

Luther, Martin. *Disputatio Heidelbergae Habita*. Vol. I of *Martin Luthers Werke. Kritische Gesamtausgabe*. Weimar: H. Böhlau, 1883.

Luz, Ulrich. "Das Jesusbild der vormarkinischen Tradition," in *Jesus Christus in Historie und Theologie:*

Neutestamentliche Festschrift für Hans Conzelmann, edited
by Georg Strecker. Tübingen: J.C.B. Mohr (Paul Siebeck),
1975, 347-374.

Ménard, Jacques-É. L'Évangile de Verité. Vol. II of Nag
Hammadi Studies, edited by M. Krause et al. Leiden:
E. J. Brill, 1972.

Menninger, Karl W. Number Words and Number Symbols: A Cultural History of Numbers. Translated by Paul Broneer
from revised German edition. Cambridge, Ma.: M.I.T.
Press, 1969.

Milik, Jozef T. The Books of Enoch: Aramaic Fragments of
Qumran Cave 4. Oxford: Clarendon Press, 1976.

Munck, Johannes. "Paul, the Apostles, and the Twelve," Studia
Theologica Cura Ordinum Theologorum Scandinavicorum, Vol.
III, Fasc. I-II (1949), 96-110.

Nestle, E. and K. Aland, eds. Novum Testamentum Graece. 26th
edition. London: United Bible Societies, 1979.

Neugebauer, Otto E. "Zodiac," Vol. 23 of Encyclopedia Britannica, Chicago: W. Benton, 1971, 982.

Nilsson, Martin P. Geschichte der Griechischen Religion.
Bd. I: Handbuch der Altertumswissenschaft. München:
C. H. Beck'sche Verlagsbuchhandlung, 1967.

Noth, Martin. Das System der Zwölf Stämme Israels. Heft 52:
Beiträge zur Wissenschaft vom Alten und Neuen Testament.
Stuttgart: W. Kohlhammer, 1930.

Perrin, Norman. Jesus and the Language of the Kingdom. Symbol
and Metaphor in New Testament Interpretation. Philadelphia:
Fortress Press, 1976.

Petersen, Norman R. Literary Criticism for New Testament
Critics. Philadelphia: Fortress Press, 1978.

Polag, Athanasius. Die Christologie der Logienquelle. No. 45:
Wissenschaftliche Monographien zum Alten und Neuen Testament. Neukirchen-Vluyn: Neukirchener Verlag, 1977.

Rad, Gerhard von. Das erste Buch Mose. 2. 3. 4. Teilband:
Das Alte Testament Deutsch. Göttingen: Vandenhoeck &
Ruprecht, 1950. 1952. 1953.

--------. Old Testament Theology. Vol. I: The Theology of
Israel's Historical Traditions. Translated by D. M. G.
Stalker. Edinburgh and London: Oliver and Boyd, 1962.

Rengstorf, Karl Heinrich. "ἀποστέλλειν etc.," in Theological Dictionary of the New Testament, Vol. 1, edited by G. Kittel. Translated by Geoffrey W. Bromiley. Grand Rapids: William B. Eerdmans, 1964, 398-447.

Rudolph, Kurt. "Simon: Magus oder Gnosticus," Theologische Rundschau, Neue Folge 42 (1977), 279-359.

Schelz, Sepp. "Umkehr am Rande des Abgrunds," Lutherische Monatshefte 19 (1980), 634-637.

Schenk, Wolfgang. "Der Einfluss der Logienquelle auf das Markusevangelium," Zeitschrift für die Neutestamentliche Wissenschaft 70 (1979), 141-165.

--------. Synopse zur Redenquelle der Evangelien: Q-Synopse und Rekonstruktion in deutscher Übersetzung mit kurzen Erläuterungen. Düsseldorf: Patmos, 1981.

Schmithals, Walter. The Office of Apostle in the Early Church. Nashville: Abingdon, 1969.

Schulz, Siegfried. Q: Die Spruchquelle der Evangelisten. Zürich: Theologischer Verlag, 1972.

Scriba, Christoph J.; with the assistance of M. E. Dormer Ellis. The Concept of Number. Hochschultaschenbücher Verlag Mannheim/Zürich: Bibliographisches Institut, 1968.

Sloyan, Gerard S. Is Christ the End of the Law? Philadelphia: Westminster Press, 1978.

Steck, Odil H. Israel und das gewaltsame Geschick der Propheten: Untersuchungen zur Überlieferung des deuteronomistischen Geschichtsbildes im Alten Testament. No. 23: Wissenschaftliche Monographien zum Neuen Testament. Neukirchen-Vluyn: Neukirchener Verlag, 1967.

Strecker, Georg. Der Weg der Gerechtigkeit: Untersuchung zur Theologie des Matthäus. 3rd edition, revised and expanded. No. 82: Forschungen zur Theologie und Literatur des Alten und Neuen Testaments. Göttingen: Vandenhoeck & Ruprecht, 1971.

Streeter. Burnett H. The Four Gospels: A Study of Origins. London: Macmillan, 1924 and 1936.

Talbert, Charles H. Luke and the Gnostics: An Examination of the Lucan Purpose. Nashville: Abingdon Press, 1966.

--------. What is a Gospel: The Genre of the Canonical Gospels. Philadelphia: Fortress Press, 1977.

Theissen, Gerd. "Wanderradikalismus. Literatursoziologische Aspekte der Überlieferung von Worten Jesu im Urchristentum," Zeitschrift für Theologie und Kirche 70 (1973), 245-271.

--------. The First Followers of Jesus. A Sociological Analysis of the Earliest Christianity. London: SCM Press, 1978.

Tödt, Heinz. The Son of Man in the Synoptic Tradition. Translated by Dorothea M. Barton. Philadelphia: Westminster, 1965. (The New Testament Library).

Vaux, Roland de. "La Thèse de l'Amphictyonie Israélite," The Harvard Theological Review 64 (1971), 415-436.

Vermes, Geza. The Dead Sea Scrolls in English. Baltimore, Md.: Penguin Books, 1962, reprinted with revisions 1965.

--------. The Dead Sea Scrolls: Qumran in Perspective. London: Collins, 1977.

--------. "The Impact of the Dead Sea Scrolls on Jewish Studies During the Last Twenty-Five Years," in Approaches to Ancient Judaism: Theory and Practice. Brown Judaic Studies I, edited by W. S. Green. Missoula, Mont.: Scholars Press, 1978.

Vielhauer, Philipp. "Speise und Trank Johannes des Täufers," Aufsätze zum Neuen Testament. Bd. 31: Theologische Bücherei. München: Kaiser Verlag, 1965, 47-54.

--------. "Gottesreich und Menschensohn in der Verkündigung Jesu," Aufsätze zum Neuen Testament. Bd. 31: Theologische Bücherei. München: Kaiser Verlag, 1965, 55-91.

Weeden, Theodore J. Mark: Traditions in Conflict. Philadelphia: Fortress Press, 1971.

Weise, Christian W. Die evangelische Geschichte: Kritisch und Philosophisch Bearbeitet. 2 Bände. Leipzig: Breitkopf und Härtel, 1838.

Wellhausen, Julius. Einleitung in die drei ersten Evangelien. Berlin: Reimer, 1905.

Westermann, Claus. Genesis. Bd. I/2: Biblischer Kommentar Altes Testament. Neukirchen-Vluyn: Neukirchener Verlag, 1981.

Wilson, Robert McLachlan. Gnosis and the New Testament. Oxford: Basil Blackwell, 1968.

Wolff, Hans Walter. "The Kerygma of the Deuteronomic Historical Work," <u>The Vitality of Old Testament Traditions</u> by
W. Brueggemann and H. W. Wolff. Atlanta: Knox Press,
1975, 83-100.

INDEX OF QUOTATIONS

A. <u>The Old Testament</u>

B. The Pseudepigrapha of the Old Testament

C. The New Testament

E. The Dead Sea Scrolls

F. The Rabbinical Sources

INDEX OF SUBJECTS

Black, David Alan

PAUL, APOSTLE OF WEAKNESS
Astheneia and its Cognates in the Pauline Literature

New York, Berne, Frankfurt/M., 1984. 340 pp.
American University Studies: Series 7, Theology and Religion. Vol. 3
ISBN 0-8204-0106-4   pb./lam. US $ 27.–

The most unique and highly developed concept of weakness in the New Testament is to be found in the writings of the apostle Paul. Essentially, Paul's conception of weakness stands in a dynamic relationship with his Christology. He is defensive of his own infirmities only because a misunderstanding of weakness has led to error concerning the nature and acquisition of divine strength. Paul is strong, but only because he is «in Christ». Otherwise he freely admits to being an apostle of weakness, and in so doing has set forth a powerful rationale for Christians of all ages to glory in their weaknesses, not merely endure them. Contents: The Weak in Thessalonica – Weakness Language in Galatians – The Pauline Perspective on Weakness – Weakness as a Sign of Humanity – Weakness as the Showplace of God's Might – Paul's Relevance for Today.

Basser, Herbert W.

MIDRASHIC INTERPRETATIONS OF THE SONG OF MOSES

New York, Berne, Frankfurt/M., 1984. 326 pp.
American University Studies: Series 7, Theology and Religion. Vol. 2
ISBN 0-8204-0065-3   pb/lam. US $ 28.85

This work provides a translation of, and a commentary to the text of *Sifre Ha'azinu*. Finkelstein's edition (1939, reprinted JTS 1969) and selected readings of the London manuscript of this midrash appear in translation with full notes covering textual observations, philological inquiries and exegetical problems. The following ideas are discussed within the course of the work: midrashic forms, the use of Scripture in midrash, the dating of the traditions and of the recording of this midrash, the use of apologetic and polemic in midrash. An *Introduction* and *Conclusion* have been provided which discuss the items in this midrash which are relevant to the academic study of Judaism. The literary aspects of this midrash on Deut. 32 are used to exemplify *midrashim* on poetic Scriptures. Contents: Introduction discussing literary, theological, historical aspects of midrash – Translation and analysis of the midrash to Deut. 32. Sifre Deuteronomy – Conclusion summing up the findings in the work.

PETER LANG PUBLISHING, INC.
34 East 39th Street, USA – New York, NY 10016